AN ESSAY ON STRATEGY

Also by Robert Neild

PRICING AND EMPLOYMENT IN THE TRADE CYCLE
THE REFORM AND MEASUREMENT OF BUDGETARY POLICY
  (*with T. S. Ward*)
HOW TO MAKE UP YOUR MIND ABOUT THE BOMB
THE FOUNDATIONS OF DEFENSIVE DEFENCE (*edited with Anders
  Boserup*)

An Essay on Strategy

as it Affects the Achievement of Peace in a Nuclear Setting

Robert Neild
Professor Emeritus of Economics, Cambridge
Fellow of Trinity College, Cambridge

MACMILLAN

First published 1990

Published by
THE MACMILLAN PRESS LTD
Houndmills, Basingstoke, Hampshire RG21 2XS
and London
Companies and representatives
throughout the world

Printed and bound in Great Britain by
WBC Ltd, Bristol and Maesteg

British Library Cataloguing in Publication Data
Neild, R. R. (Robert Ralph), *1924–*
An essay on strategy as it affects the achievement of
peace in a nuclear setting.
1. Peace, Maintenance, Role of weapons
I. Title
327.1′72
ISBN 0–333–52986–3 (hardcover)
ISBN 0–333–52987–1 (paperback)

Contents

Contents

To my children

Preface

I must first acknowledge an unusual debt. It is to Anders Boserup. He and I set out to write this book together about five years ago. After more than a year of often intense work, when we had produced the core of the first few chapters, we decided to give up the collaboration and work separately. We did not disagree over any major point of substance, but gaps remained to be filled, and there was too wide a gulf between our approaches, between his instinct and astonishing capacity to carry the process of logical and methodological dissection always a stage further and my English instinct to halt when I feel I have reached a formulation that is logically adequate to the problem in hand. After an interval of about two years, we both felt that a book setting out this body of ideas was badly needed, and I, with his encouragement, decided to go ahead on my own, making full use of the work we had done together. I had hoped that when he had seen the resulting draft he might feel able to add his name to mine as co-author, but his reservations about my treatment of some points were such that he felt he could not do so, and it was too late to start a new attempt at an agreed text. Anders Boserup contributed many of the most important ideas to the chapters on theory in the first part of the book. My debt to him is immeasurable.

He and I are together editing a collection of papers, including some by each of us, which deal more fully with some of the issues raised in this essay. The papers are drawn principally from the Pugwash Workshop on Conventional Defence in Europe. The collection, entitled *The Foundations of Defensive Defence*, is also published by Macmillan.

I have benefitted from many discussions of one of the main topics addressed in this essay – alternative strategies for non-nuclear defence in Europe – with civilian and military experts from East and West whom I have met at the Pugwash Workshop, at seminars in Moscow convened by Professor Andrey Kokoshin and Dr Evgeni Silin, and at seminars in Bavaria organised by Dr Albrecht von Müller under the auspices of the newly-formed European Centre for International Security.

I am indebted to Field Marshal Lord Carver and Dr Oliver Ramsbotham, who read the whole of this essay in draft, and to Professor Norman Stone and Mrs Darrah, who read the Historical

Appendix. They offered most valuable comments. For errors that remain and for the views expressed I am wholly responsible. Finally, I must express my gratitude to Adèle Simmons and to students and members of the faculities of the five colleges at Amherst on whom I was able to try some of the substance of this essay at an early stage, and to Tina Bone for typing and helping with the problems of using a word processor.

Trinity College   ROBERT NEILD
Cambridge

Acknowledgements

The author and publishers wish to thank the author and Oxford University Press for permission to reproduce copyright material from Arthur J. Marder, *From the Dreadnought to Scapa Flow: The Royal Navy in the Fisher Era. 1904 to 1919*, Vol. 1, *The Road to War* (1961); and The Macmillan Press Ltd for permission to reproduce copyright material from Frederick W. Holls, *The Peace Conference at the Hague and its Bearing on International Law and Policy.*

1 Introduction

Strategy is the art of pursuing political aims by the use or possession of military means. In formulating strategy, the first step is to decide on political aims. Without political aims, war is mindless destruction and the possession of military means in peacetime is mindless waste. Once political aims are specified, the military means must be selected and tailored to fit those aims.

This definition of strategy, which derives from Clausewitz, is not something which anyone would dispute.[1] But it has been lost to view – or at least not been clearly in the foreground – since military thinking became concentrated on nuclear weapons. Under the label 'Deterrence', a military means, namely the making of threats to keep your potential enemy at bay, has taken the place of a political aim. Policies have been advocated on the grounds that they will 'strengthen deterrence' as if that was a political aim rather than a means of achieving an aim.

Moreover, what has passed for a theory of deterrence, meaning a theory which, in a nuclear stalemate, would tell you how to achieve your political aims, has been a body of thought which, as we shall see, has lacked logical coherence. The advocates of a new weapons systems, or a new deployment, have been able to use one set of arguments drawn from the theory to make their case; their opponents have been able to use another set of arguments drawn from the same body of thought to oppose the case; and the issue has been settled, not by a logical resolution of the arguments, but in response to extraneous factors, for example, the relative strength of the lobbies commanded by the two sides; the urgency with which the weapons laboratories and arms firms, which the government wishes to keep in being, need new work; the swing of the political pendulum.

That these extraneous factors have been important, not to say dominant, has often been recognised. And many thoughtful experts – for example, Brodie, Freedman and Jervis – have seen that what now passes for a theory of nuclear strategy is not satisfactory. They have not, however, offered anything to put in its place.[2]

The suggestion of this essay is that the way forward is to reconsider theory from first principles, starting from political aims and then considering what are the alternative military strategies that fit those aims and how they can be implemented. The theoretical framework is

1

general, but the analysis is concentrated on the question how best to achieve peace in the presence of nuclear weapons.

THE IMPORTANCE OF THEORY

Theories are propositions about cause and effect. They determine what we think about how the world works. We may take a theory for granted, for example, the law of gravity, but it will still be there guiding our actions and our reasoning. If, as is now the case with nuclear strategy, you can reach contradictory conclusions from the existing theory, for example, if one person using the theory of gravity could conclude that if you let go of an object it would go upwards and another could reach the conclusion that it would go downwards, you would have on your hands a defective theory, useless as a guide to action.

Theoretical reasoning is peculiarly important in the formulation of military strategy, because war, which is the practical test of strategy, occurs only at intervals. In normal activities, for example the production of motor cars, the product flows forth and is put to the test by consumers every day; the producer continuously learns if his product is any good. But the output of the military is war, and that is not produced and put to the test every day. If the political aim is to avoid war, the greater the success in achieving that aim, the greater the remoteness in time of the last war and hence of any concrete experience to go by. Strategy is then bound to be based on traditional beliefs that were last fully tested in conditions that may have become irrelevant and on theories that are untested except by simulations, war games, military exercises and, possibly, by the observation of wars in other parts of the world. As war is avoided, strategy becomes more and more 'academic'. And as that happens it becomes more and more important to look critically at the prevailing theories. This applies with particular force to nuclear weapons. Since the aim of nuclear strategy is to avoid the use of nuclear weapons, nuclear strategy cannot rest on anything but theory – so long as it is successful. Only if it failed and there was a nuclear war, would there be any evidence to go by.

The re-examination of theory will be divided into three chapters, dealing in turn with political aims, nuclear strategy, and sub-nuclear strategy.

The purpose, as in any theoretical analysis, is to establish deductive connections among concepts and among propositions so as to ensure that we reason in a coherent way. A second consideration is relevance: the theory should represent the real world in a useful way. For that purpose evidence will be touched upon.

Nations and alliances will frequently be spoken of as if they were single persons choosing political aims and reckoning what was the best way of achieving those aims through the possession or use of military means. There are two grounds for doing this. In the first place, it is the way that people usually think about these problems. Secondly, it is a procedure which permits you to see the logical connections between ends and means, and to see the effect that one nation's actions may have on the perceptions and actions of another; it helps to clarify the alternatives open to policy-makers; it provides a basis on which to assess the policies that have been followed.

But of course nations and alliances are not individuals; their policies emerge with inertia from complex political processes in which many groups offer advice and bring pressure to bear; in which leaders seek not to lose face; in which opinion is influenced by the public relations efforts of the military and the arms firms, by the flow of expertise offered by the strategic analysts and also by the views offered by peace researchers and the peace movements and many others. We do not hope to trace these causes. We seek only to see what were the dominant arguments and thrusts of policy. But the processes beneath the surface should not be forgotten.

The argument that the present theory of nuclear strategy – usually called deterrence theory – is not coherent, which we shall develop in Chapter 3, is often met by the rejoinder, 'But deterrence works: we haven't had a war'. That is true, and one cannot doubt that the existence of nuclear weapons has contributed, by inducing caution, to the avoidance of war. But that does not mean that the strategies the nuclear powers have adopted and the nuclear arsenals they have acquired have been the product of a coherent theory. It does not mean that there are grounds for believing that, if we had had nuclear arsenals of quite different size, composition and balance, we would not have avoided war just as well. The period since 1945 to which the claim that 'deterrence works' is applied, has witnessed a United States nuclear monopoly with a few weapons, followed by huge United States numerical superiority over the Soviet Union, then a diminishing lead as the Soviet Union caught up, and then 'parity' at the grotesque level of about 25,000 warheads each. Meanwhile nuclear weapons have spread to a number of other nations. If deterrence has worked in all these situations, deterrence means almost anything. To say that nuclear weapons have induced caution and so helped to keep the peace is quite consistent with the statement that we have been suffering from a lack of a coherent theory about what to do with nuclear weapons.

Finally, a qualification. It is increasingly doubtful, for reasons which have little or nothing to do with nuclear weapons, whether wars can be won, in the classical sense that the will of one side to fight can be broken, after which his territory and people can be ruled by the victor. The growth of nationalism, the ending of passive ignorance and the ready access of all peoples to small arms and explosives make the subjugation of foreign peoples to military conquest and occupation increasingly problematical. Vietnam, Afghanistan, Palestine and Northern Ireland are examples. This trend, which is likely to continue, is invalidating the classical notion of decisive victory, and seems to be producing a militarily more Maoist world.

At the same time, economic and technical progress is making it hard to visualise how a long non-nuclear war in Europe (assuming away nuclear weapons for the moment), or any other modern urbanised area, could be sustained, or what it would be like. The ability of nations to bombard one another accurately is increasing, while the ability of modern urban societies to withstand bombardment is decreasing. If, for example, electricity is cut off from a modern city there will be neither water nor drainage; all the lifts, heating, air conditioning, refrigerators and freezers will stop in houses, offices, shops, warehouses and factories; railways and traffic signals will cease to work; computers that control many aspects of economic life will stop. The more advanced the city the more vulnerable it will be to paralysis, starvation and infection, unless extraordinary preparations are made.[3] On the battlefield, the rate of use of ammunition and the rate of destruction of fighting vehicles and equipment experienced in recent wars in the Middle East have been so high that the war has either been brought to an end; or there have been forced lulls, for example, in the Iran–Iraq war, during which each side has attempted to re-equip itself.

2 The Political Level

POLITICAL AIMS AND MILITARY MEANS

That war should be subordinate to politics is a principle from which strategic analysis starts and from which it must never depart. From it flows the definition of strategy as the study of a means of achieving political ends, as an art, a know-how.

For this principle to be fulfilled the strategy and the military forces of a nation must be chosen, trained and deployed in such a way that in a crisis, or in the midst or war, 'military necessity' does not come into conflict with political prudence nor compel political leaders to accept actions that are politically less acceptable than an alternative strategy for which preparations might have been made. War should never be allowed blindly to follow its own course, driven by a logic of war or a notion of military effectiveness not articulated by reference to political aims. This does not mean that considerations of military effectiveness should be set aside. On the contrary, it is to insist that true military effectiveness should be achieved, after political considerations have given meaning to that term.

In practice this is not easy to achieve. Military staffs have to make plans for the military operations they may be called upon to conduct; they, together with intelligence staffs and foreign affairs departments, must advise their political masters – typically the Prime Minister (or President), the Minister for Defence and the Minister for Foreign Affairs, and one or two trusted advisers – on what they see as the main political-cum-military threats – or opportunities – for which preparations should or might be made. The political masters may take the initiative and seek military adventures or retrenchment. Whether they do that or not, they carry the responsibility for making the choices, i.e. for deciding what political aims to choose in the light of the professional advice offered. Having done that, they will then have to depend in large measure on their military staffs for advice on what kinds of strategies, forces and weapons should be chosen in order to achieve the chosen political aims. What they choose will constitute the military programme of the nation, a programme that cannot be changed rapidly since there are long 'lead-times' between decisions to acquire weapons and train forces and the readiness of those weapons and forces for operations.

When nuclear weapons are present, the problem of ensuring that the military means of a nation are geared to its political aims assumes a new character and a quite new importance.

DIFFERENT SETTINGS

The difference between conditions when nuclear weapons are present and conditions when they are not is central to our analysis and needs to be defined precisely. For this purpose, we shall refer to a 'nuclear setting' and a 'classical setting'.

We shall say that there is a *nuclear setting* when two nations possess, and know each other to possess, sufficient nuclear weapons for each to have the capacity to do unacceptable damage to the other side, after allowing for possible losses of weapons and weapon failures. It is a condition that has been called the possession of the capability for MAD (mutual assured destruction). This is a condition that will exist when two nations possess invulnerable weapons of any kind that have the capacity to do unacceptable damage. Nuclear weapons may be just the precursors of many weapons with that capacity. As a class, we could call them 'terminal weapons', and we could talk about a 'terminal setting'. We shall stick to the terms nuclear weapons and nuclear setting since they will be more familiar to the reader; but the wider meaning should not be forgotten.

A *classical setting* exists when neither side possesses terminal weapons or where one side only possesses them.

ENDS AND MEANS IN THE CLASSICAL SETTING

It is best to go back to Clausewitz, whose ideas on the relationship between political ends and the use of military means were seminal.

Clausewitz starts from the assertion that war is an instrument of politics, a mere continuation of politics by other means. It can well be argued that the best way to define those means, and thus arrive at a general definition of war, is to say that war is the resort to the unconstrained use of *any* means, including military force, that serve the attainment of the political aim; that what characterises the act of going to war and the conduct of war is the abandonment of constraint. But Clausewitz followed a different line of reasoning, a line appropriate to the setting he was considering but less general and not suitable for application to a nuclear setting. He concentrated on the nature of the military aims pursued in war. The foundation of his theory is the distinction between the political purpose of a war and the military aim in a war.

A nation may go to war in pursuit of various political purposes, for example, to topple a government, to acquire territory or to open a trade route. But once war is declared, these purposes are replaced by the single aim of winning the war, meaning achieving victory and avoiding defeat, those being two sides of a single coin. The political purposes of the two belligerents may be strictly opposite or they may merely be different in some lesser degree, but their war aims are always and necessarily polar opposites: victory for one is defeat for the other.

The idea that there is a single war aim, independent of the political purposes of wars, the same for everyone and in all wars, has important implications.

It means first of all that strategic calculus in war has a logic all its own that sets it apart from strategic calculus in the realm of politics. In politics there is always a plurality of goals that are being pursued simultaneously. The use of some particular means will generally have implications for several of the goals, and the main task of political strategy therefore consists in making value judgements, deciding what is an acceptable compromise between goals that are neither fully compatible nor directly comparable. In war in a classical framework, on the other hand, there is a single criterion by which to assess alternative actions. A course of action may have both beneficial and detrimental effects but it is always possible, in principle, to compare these effects, to determine their combined, net effect because there is a single criterion by which to make a judgement: does it bring victory closer – or push defeat away?

So long as this was so, it made sense to establish military institutions, from High Commands downward, that have a high degree of autonomy, subject to political control as to the political purposes for which the military forces should be prepared and used.

A second feature of the classical setting has been a simple relationship between the war aim (to prevail in battle) and the means used (force). Once war starts and force is resorted to, there is a trial of strength; the more force the better. In the classical setting it has been possible to imagine that there is an inherent 'logic of war', a logic of the use of force, which, generally speaking, determines the meaning of 'military effectiveness'. The amount of force is the measure of effectiveness: the greater the available force, the more effective the military instrument. Military planners will have done their job if they have provided the greatest amount of force that can be obtained with the economic resources and choice of techniques available to them.

This is still commonly true where nuclear weapons and their shadow are absent, where classical conditions obtain. But even in a classical setting, crude non-nuclear destructive power, which nowadays can be obtained in abundance by rich nations, may not be a reliable means of obtaining victory (Chapter 1); and in a nuclear setting, ends and means, and the relationship between them, are very different.

The fact that in a classical setting military strength is put to the test without constraint means that threats can be effective. If you are confident that you are stronger than your opponent, you can threaten him for the sake of a political concession without inhibition and, if he refuses to yield, you can execute the threat by unleashing your forces at him. By the same token, if the other side judges that it is weaker, it can surrender.

If one side possesses nuclear weapons, the basic conditions of the classical setting still hold. The political aims of the nation that possesses nuclear weapons will not be constrained by the fear of a nuclear exchange. It can use its nuclear weapons to threaten attack and, if need be, to attack, without fear of retaliation. The nation without nuclear weapons faces an adversary who enjoys superior nuclear-cum-non-nuclear military strength and who can use that strength just as it would use non-nuclear strength – subject to the special political inhibitions that may attach to the use of nuclear weapons. These are important and are discussed in Chapter 3.

ENDS AND MEANS IN A NUCLEAR SETTING

In a nuclear setting the fact that any military engagement between the two nuclear participants can escalate to an all-out nuclear exchange constrains the political purposes for which the use of military power can be entertained. The political purposes for which military forces are built up and deployed become the prevention of war, the preservation of the status quo, or the pursuit of such political gains as a risk-taker thinks he may be able to achieve without provoking war. That strategy would be constrained in this way was seen in the early days of nuclear weapons by Bernard Brodie. In 1946 he wrote 'Thus far the chief purpose of our military establishment has been to win wars. From now on its chief purpose must be to avert them. It can have almost no other useful purpose.[1]

The implications of this change in the political purposes for which the use of military force can be entertained are several and important.

The first is that if war should occur at the sub-nuclear level, the military aim should not be victory in decisive non-nuclear battle. To pursue such an aim is to attempt to create a situation in which the loser, be it the enemy or your own side, is faced by decisive defeat of his non-nuclear forces. To avoid political surrender, he may be driven to use nuclear weapons, so starting a nuclear exchange that nullifies any possible political gain to either side. To avoid this, the military aim, imposed by the supreme political dictate of survival, becomes the propagation of stalemate on present frontiers – or possibly after gaining a slice of territory or some other asset (Chapter 4).

The second implication is that the amount of military force, measured in destructive power, that the armed forces of a nation can wield is no longer a measure of their effectiveness as a military instrument. There is a saturation point, beyond which destructive power can be excessive and may be counter-productive of the nation's political purposes.

The third implication is that the design of military forces must be dictated by political considerations far more closely than before. Political reasoning must enter the planning, procurement and deployment of military forces in a way that has no place in a classical setting. Thus instead of the classical dictum that more force means more effectiveness of the armed forces for the task of pursuing the political purposes of the nation, it may be necessary in a nuclear setting to adopt the dictum that the better are the non-nuclear forces at propagating a stalemate, winning time and avoiding battle, the better they will be able to achieve the political purposes of the nation in a nuclear setting. And if a nuclear nation operates sometimes in a nuclear setting, facing nations that do not possess nuclear weapons, and perhaps sometimes in between, facing the allies of nuclear nations, it is all the more important that political reasoning and supervision should be brought to bear so as to ensure that for each setting the military make preparations and take actions appropriate to the political purposes that can be pursued within that setting. Preparations and actions must be avoided which suggest that what is appropriate to one setting will be carried out in another where it is not appropriate.

The fourth implication is that in a nuclear setting the military instrument at the disposal of policy is not the act of war but the making and remaking of preparations for war: the processes of acquiring arms and forces, deploying them, setting forth doctrines for their use, and issuing implicit and explicit warnings and threats; and, when political reconciliation is being pursued, the process of easing those threats and making preparations for defence that are as reassuring as possible to the other side. It is through wise decisions at this level that policy can try to achieve the desired goals.

The problem of how, in a nuclear setting, to shape preparations for war so that political aims are achieved is complicated by two considerations: there is no longer a general criterion of strength by reference to which investments in forces can be made; and, secondly, the political purposes, and the military aims that are consistent with those purposes, vary according as the setting for which preparations are made is nuclear, classical or in the grey area in between. The stability of your force becomes a prime criterion, and so does the 'feedback' of your actions on those of your potential opponents: you must give up the blind pursuit of 'strength' and consider how the other side will react in the short run and in the long run.

STABILITY

Strategy and the structure of military forces can be unstable, meaning that one military move by you or your potential enemy, or even an unintended incident, may lead to another in a manner that gets out of control. There are two main types of instability – crisis instability and escalation instability.

A classic example of crisis instability is 1914. The military plans and chains of command were such that, once the crisis had been started by the murder of the Austrian archduke, a race to mobilise and be ready to attack first was started between the rival powers, a race which rapidly gathered momentum, with the result that, 'The rush to the abyss now gathered unbreakable speed – driven by the motor of "military necessity".[2] This does not mean that the outbreak of war was unintended politically. Rather, a political readiness to go to war was one reason why irreversible plans for competitive mobilisation were established and were then set in motion.

Nowadays a new form of crisis instability associated with modern weaponry has also become important. The advent of highly effective offensive weapons – aircraft, missiles and armoured forces – that are capable of attacking the similar weapons of the other side and are also vulnerable to attack by them, has produced a new and more potent variant of the temptation to attack first. If on land each side has parked aircraft, missiles or concentrations of armoured forces that are vulnerable, each will think, 'If I do not knock out his forces first, he will knock out mine' and, knowing that the other side will be thinking likewise they may each become more nervous and feel an increasing necessity to take the initiative and attack first – or, to put it in the jargon, to make a 'pre-emptive attack'. The same kind of pressure to attack pre-emptively applies to nuclear weapons, if they are vulnerable to a 'first strike'.

Escalation instability concerns the transition from non-nuclear to nuclear war. If, for example, the non-nuclear strategy chosen by two opposed nations is the pursuit of decisive victory in mobile armoured warfare, it is likely that in the event of war one side will suffer a decisive defeat at the non-nuclear level and will then have no choice but to escalate to the use of nuclear weapons or surrender. Escalation instability will be a consequence of the non-nuclear strategies and force structures chosen by the two sides.

FEEDBACK

Feedback is the effect that the strategy of one side in a confrontation has on the political perceptions, the strategy and the military programme of the other, including the size of its future military spending. Consider a confrontation between two non-nuclear nations. Suppose the aims of one of the nations are peaceful and suppose further that geography and technology permit some choice between a more defensive and a more offensive strategy and force structure. Suppose the military experts judge that, without a great difference in expenditure, they can achieve equal security with either strategy. The political leaders will have to consider what political signal they wish to send to the other side. Do they wish to threaten him, frighten him and suggest hostility? Do they wish to adopt an aggressive posture of that kind for home consumption? If so, the more offensive strategy will be appropriate. Or do they wish to reassure their opponent, calm him, and induce reconciliation? Do they wish to adopt a peaceful posture for home consumption? If so, the more defensive strategy will be appropriate.

The political choice between the two strategies – and the choice made as to the level of forces – will influence the military strategy and the level of spending of the other side, to which the first side will in turn have to react. In this way the choice of the character and level of forces will influence the political climate and the direction and the intensity of the competition in arms between the two sides.

In general terms, feedback concerns how your choice of strategy and force structure influences your opponent's choice of strategy and forces, and *vice versa*. It expresses itself over time. Stability concerns how the strategy and forces you have adopted, and those of your opponent, influence what happens in a crisis or in war. It expresses itself at a moment in time.

The next step is to consider the main alternative strategies that can be adopted in order to achieve national political aims and assess their stability and feedback properties.

TERMINOLOGY

The main terms we use (political aims, military strategy, military stance and force structure) are defined as we go along. Readers should be warned, however, that military terms of this kind do not have standard agreed meanings; each author gives them his own meaning; national military authorities may lay down standard meanings, but these differ from country to country and, in particular, from East to West.

Perhaps the worst problem is the word doctrine, which we shall use in later chapters when we discuss the implementation of alternative strategies and analyse the evolution of the strategies and military plans of NATO (North Atlantic Treaty Organisation) and the WTO (Warsaw Treaty Organisation).

In the West, doctrine does not have a rigorous meaning. It is used only intermittently and with varying meaning. It is sometimes a general description of the spirit and manner in which it is envisaged an army would fight should there be a war. For example, historians discuss how far the French army followed an offensive doctrine before 1914 and a defensive doctrine in the inter-war period; and they discuss the relative importance of offensive and defensive doctrine in the Royal Air Force in the inter-war period. But this is a classification by inference after the event. At the time the military may never have used the word doctrine, and their contingency plans for war may have rested on little more than tradition inherited from past wars; the coherence of thought implied by the word doctrine may have been lacking.[3]

In the post-war period, however, the word doctrine has assumed greater importance in the West. Nuclear weapons are so destructive, and reliance on them has been so great in NATO, that it has been necessary to produce a formula that indicates in what circumstances they might be used. The formula has had to generate uncertainty and fear in the minds of the authorities in the East and yet be politically acceptable in the West, where it has had to reassure the European members of NATO without tying the hands of the United States authorities. The word doctrine has fitted the bill, perhaps because no one knows quite what it means. The results have been the Doctrine of Massive Retaliation and later the Doctrine of Flexible Response (Chapter 6).

In the Soviet Union and, consequently, in the Warsaw Pact, the word doctrine has a standard, elaborately-defined meaning and great importance is attached to it. It is a total military philosophy which combines an ideological, Marxist–Leninist, approach and a pragmatic approach as to how a socialist state should prepare itself for war. Thus military doctrine is formally defined as 'the established system of views of the state at a given time on the aims and character of a possible war, on the preparation of the country and armed forces for war and also on the methods of waging it.'[4] It implies the formulation of a consistent hierarchy of objectives and means of achieving those objectives from the top political and economic level down to the tactical level.

The difference in the way the word doctrine is used in the East and the West is acknowledged on both sides. Thus Alexei Arbatov, a Soviet analyst, remarks that 'The United States and other Western countries use this term [doctrine] quite arbitrarily, often employing it to designate totally different ideas'; and Christopher Donnelly, a British expert on Soviet military affairs, states that 'In matters of defence, the Soviet approach is conditioned by their concept of doctrine, which enforces a logical framework of thought on generals and politicians alike. . . NATO has no equivalent concept of doctrine. What NATO calls its "doctrine", the Soviets call "plans"'![5]

The fact that the East has a much more coherent and formal approach to doctrine than the West does not mean that it is necessarily easier to know what is the doctrine of the East, nor that doctrine is always more coherent in the East than in the West. Within their formal framework the Soviets may make compromises and muddles – indeed in the years before they were attacked by Germany they seem clearly to have done so; and in the West military planning in some countries and at some times may have been extremely coherent and efficient even though the word doctrine was not prominent, or even present, in the vocabulary.

We shall use the word doctrine in the Western manner to describe what kind of forces and plans a nation or alliance possesses for use in the event of war, paying particular attention to the distinction between defensive and offensive doctrine. The military doctrine, so defined, will be reflected in, and can be inferred from, the force structure and military stance of a nation or alliance, but is not an adequate indicator of political intentions.

ALTERNATIVE STRATEGIES: NON-NUCLEAR FORCES

It is possible, within limits, to make plans, to equip, train and deploy *non-nuclear* forces and to prepare positions, infrastructure and logistics with the emphasis on the ability to undertake offensive operations or defensive operations. How great is the choice will depend on the geography of the area where the possible war might occur and on the technology of the period (Chapter 4).

The choice between emphasis on offence and emphasis on defence in military planning has important implications for stability and feedback.

Consider first the choice of non-nuclear forces when two nations face each other in a classical setting.

Suppose that geography and technology permit you a significant choice between offensive and defensive forces. If your aims are offensive, for example, you are Napoleon or Hitler, you will go for forces that are designed with an offensive capability and are big enough to give you *offensive superiority*, meaning a high probability of winning. As we shall see, this does not mean that the forces have no defensive capability at the operational and tactical level, any more than a defensive strategy means you have zero offensive capability.

On the other hand, if your aims are peaceful, you have two methods by which you can dissuade a neighbour whom you mistrust from attacking you. One method is to threaten him with the prospect that, if he attacks you, you will attack him in return. In other words, you dissuade him by the threat of *retaliation*. This requires that your military plans and the chracteristics of your forces be offensive and visibly so: the more visible your offensive capability the better will you be able by this method to dissuade your neighbour from attacking you. It also requires that your forces must be of such a size and quality *vis-à-vis* your opponent's forces, that they visibly have a good prospect of achieving victory.

The alternative is to present to your opponent the prospect that if he attacks you he will meet resistance that will bog him down in a costly war of attrition, possibly including counter-attacks in which he is driven back to the frontier. Your opponent is dissuaded from attack by the prospect that the costs will be high and that he is likely to be denied victory: he is unlikely to be able to break your will to go on fighting. With this method the prospect that he will be denied his objectives is not associated, or is associated as little as possible, with the threat of retaliation. A strategy of *denial* requires that so far as possible your military plans and the characteristics of your forces are defensive and visibly so; and it requires that they be of such a size and quality relative to your opponent's forces that they give you a good prospect of success. You must go for *defensive superiority*.

THE DISTINCTION BETWEEN OFFENCE AND DEFENCE

The difference between offence and defence can be described in two ways. One is that the defence means protecting territory or some other asset, e.g. a ship or aircraft, whilst offence means advancing and taking territory or taking or destroying an asset other than territory. The other is that defence means being passive, waiting for attack, whilst offence means taking the initiative, moving first.

It is tempting to adopt one of these definitions and reject the other, but to do so would probably increase rather than reduce confusion. For example, if we adopted the second definition and excluded the first, we would have to say that strategic nuclear missiles are defensive if they are intended only for retaliation; and we would have difficulty knowing what to call weapons designed to intercept and destroy strategic nuclear missiles. Are they offensive because they frustrate defence by threat of retaliation? Or are they defensive because you do not take the initiative with them but wait for attack before launching them? The confusion we shall generate if, as is customary, we use the words defence and offence sometimes with

one meaning sometimes the other, according to context, seems likely
to be less than if we rigidly adopt one meaning. But the fact that there
are these two meanings should be kept in mind.

THE CHOICE BETWEEN OFFENSIVENESS AND DEFENSIVENESS

The implications of the argument so far is this: if two countries (or
alliances) face each other in a classical setting, their choice between
emphasis on the offensive and defensive should depend on political
considerations. If their intentions are aggressive, they must emphasise the offensive; they must seek offensive superiority. If their
aims are peaceful, they can either seek to dissuade the other side by
threat of retaliation, which means they should go for offensive
superiority; or they can seek to dissuade the other side from attack by
the prospect of denial, which means they should seek defensive
superiority.

The most elementary – and often ignored – political consideration
is that if a nation or alliance whose aims are peaceful adopts a
strategy of dissuasion by retaliation, it will adopt the same kind of
offensive doctrine and will visibly possess the same kind of forces as it
would if its aims were offensive. By doing so, it is likely to make the
other side fear that its aims are offensive, not peaceful. Country A
may declare to Country B repeatedly that its aims are peaceful, but B
is not likely to heed A's words alone and ignore the message
conveyed by A's force structure. If that indicates that A has a strong
offensive capability, B will wonder whether A's words, like Hitler's
before he attacked his neighbours, may not be calculated to soothe
and mislead; or whether the present leader of A may not be replaced
by a successor with hostile intentions. The existence of an offensive
force structure, which will be visible to B and cannot be changed
quickly, will carry weight, whatever A's words. The point is illustrated in Figure 2.1.

Figure 2.1   Aims, Strategy, Stance and Structure: the choices
available – non-nuclear level

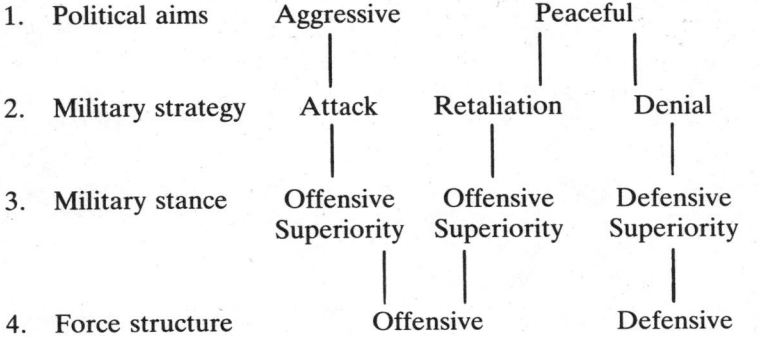

1. Political aims   Aggressive   Peaceful

2. Military strategy   Attack   Retaliation   Denial

3. Military stance   Offensive   Offensive   Defensive
                         Superiority   Superiority   Superiority

4. Force structure   Offensive   Defensive

Line 1 shows the alternative political aims – aggressive or peaceful. Line 2 shows the alternative military strategies consistent with those political aims: attack if your aim is aggressive, retaliation *or* denial if your aim is peaceful. Line 3 shows the military stance appropriate to those strategies: offensive superiority if your aim is attack or retaliation, defensive superiority if your aim is denial. Line 4 shows the force structures appropriate to each strategy: offensive forces for attack and retaliation, defensive forces for denial. Read downward like this, the figure shows step by step the choices open to you if your aims are aggressive or peaceful.

But your potential enemy will read it the other way up. He will start from the force structure that is visible to him, i.e. at the bottom of the figure, and work upwards. Above an 'Offensive' force structure, there are two lines and they lead him to aggressive or peaceful aims; above a 'Defensive' force structure there is one line and it leads him only to peaceful aims.

THE INTERACTION OF DEFENSIVE AND OFFENSIVE STRATEGIES

The next step is to consider what is the effect of the choice of strategies made by two nations (or alliances) upon the stability and feedback. To take a highly simplified example, suppose the two sides could engage only in land warfare and could possess only two kinds of forces, tank forces (mobile and of high offensive capability), and anti-tank minefields (immobile and highly defensive). If they each had a mixture of tanks and minefields of equal size and the chances of either succeeding if they attacked was 50:50 (with a margin of uncertainty), we could say that the offensive capability of each side equalled its defensive capability: the two sides possessed all-round forces and were of equal strength.

Suppose that both sides decided to go for defensive strategies and got rid of all their tanks whilst keeping their minefields, each would find that its defensive capability (its unchanged minefields) exceeded the offensive capability of the other side (which with no tanks would be zero). Both sides would enjoy defensive superiority; there would be *Mutual Defensive Superiority*. Suppose that on the contrary both sides went for offensive strategies and got rid of their minefields and kept only their tanks, then the result would be that each, owing to the potential advantages of surprise attack, would have a greater probability of winning than losing if it attacked the other. Each would enjoy offensive superiority, there would be *Mutual Offensive Superiority*. Finally, one side, perhaps because it was a much larger nation, might enjoy both defensive and offensive superiority. There would be *One-sided Dominance*.* (see box opposite.)

The main stability and feedback properties of these alternative combined stances (which are analysed more fully in Chapter 4) are these.

One-sided dominance, whatever its political properties, is militarily stable so long as the weaker power, which is too small to rival its powerful neighbour by procuring more arms, does not challenge its neighbour by making alliances that seem threatening to the neighbour.

Mutual Offensive Superiority is likely to cause crisis instability, in the form of pressure for pre-emptive attack; and escalation instability, since the pursuit of decisive battle goes with the possession of mobile offensive forces; and it will produce negative feedback in the form of political fear and competitive arming.

Mutual Defensive Superiority should produce crisis stability: the smaller the offensive capabilities of the two sides relative to each other's defensive capabilities, the less will be their ability to attack, the less will they fear attack and the less will they feel pressure to attack. Escalation stability will be improved since decisive battle need not be part of a defensive strategy. And feedback will be favourable: the military stances of the two sides are reassuring and the pressure to arm competitively will diminish and become negative.

---

*The three military stances can be depicted by writing D for the defensive capability and O for the offensive capability of countries A and B, denoting the countries by subscripts: D_A is the defensive capability of A, D_B is the defensive capability of B, and so on.[6] If we start from a situation where each nation has 'all-round' forces, meaning that their offensive capabilities and defensive capabilities are equal, we have

$$D_A = O_A$$
$$D_A = O_B$$

Suppose further that there is a balance of forces, meaning that the forces of the two sides are equally strong, we have

$$D_A = O_A = D_B = O_B$$

We can take this as a common starting point for analytical purposes, though as we shall see later, this does not mean that the pursuit of balance in all-round forces is a neutral or desirable military stance to adopt.

Defensive superiority for A is $D_A > O_B$ and defensive superiority for B is $D_B > O_A$. Mutual Defensive Superiority is $D_A > O_B$, $D_B > O_A$.

Offensive superiority for A is $O_A > D_B$, and offensive superiority for B is $O_B > D_A$. Mutual Offensive Superiority is $O_A > D_B$, $O_B > D_A$.

One-sided dominance $O_A > D_B$, $D_A > O_B$.

The last point needs amplification. The adoption of defensiveness will reduce and reverse the competitive pressure to arm not just because it eases political fear and mistrust but because the military necessity to keep up with your neighbour in arms is diminished as military stances become defensive: the more the character of your military forces is defensive, the less need your neighbour worry about their size. To take the same simple example as before, if you introduced minefields, which are inherently immobile and passive, and progressively reduced your tank forces, your neighbour would not mind how many mines you laid; as you reduced your tanks, which were the only threat to him, he could reduce his military spending. If, finally, you had nothing but minefields, he would not need to spend anything on military forces, regardless of the size of your minefields. In short, with defensiveness, the arms race feedback becomes downward rather than upward.

THE IMPLICATIONS FOR BALANCE AND FORCE LEVELS

It can readily be seen that the common view that a balance of military strength with your potential enemy is the necessary condition of security needs to be re-examined and so does the view that to negotiate balanced reductions in forces is the way to increase security and end an arms race.

We consider these points here with reference to non-nuclear forces, later with reference to nuclear forces.

We have seen that if your potential opponent were to arm himself only with purely defensive means (minefields) you would not have to react by arming in order to safeguard your security. But the greater the offensive capability of forces he chooses the more will you have to react to his arming by arming yourself. It follows that how closely you have to pursue balance in arms is a function of how far your opponent's forces have an offensive capability; and how far he has to react to your forces depends on how far your forces have an offensive capability. *It is the offensiveness of the non-nuclear forces chosen – and offensive forces may or may not be avoidable – that is the military cause of competition to acquire arms.*

Yet – and this is perhaps the more important point – if forces are offensive, a balance of forces will not yield stability and security. For, the combined stance that results is Mutual Offensive Superiority, or something approaching it, and that combined stance, as we have seen, produces crisis instability, escalation instability and negative feedback.

So we can say that *offensiveness in the character of forces produces the pursuit of balance and also causes instability and adverse feedback when forces are balanced.*

Since balanced offensive forces, which will often be perceived to be unbalanced, produce instability and adverse feedback, it follows that a balanced change in the magnitude of those forces cannot be relied upon to increase or decrease stability nor to improve feedback (Chapter 5). It is true that a change in the level of forces may change the relative strengths of defence and offence. For example, as the level of forces is reduced, the attacker's forces can more easily be picked off by the defenders; or, perhaps at another lower level, the defender's forces may be so thinly dispersed that the attacker can more easily find ways through them (Chapter 4). But these are second-order, indirect effects; they are changes in the relative effectiveness of defence and offence consequent on changes in the level of forces. In order to improve stability – and feedback – and hence enhance security, it is necessary to consider from the start what *qualitative* changes in military stances and force structures are needed and then consider the relationship between qualitative changes and reductions – or increases – in the quantity of forces required to achieve political aims. In short, qualitative change in the direction of defensiveness is the way to stability, favourable feedback and arms reductions; and *vice versa.*

WAYS TO MUTUAL DEFENSIVE SUPERIORITY

If you start with balanced all-round non-nuclear forces, which we shall again use as a benchmark, a move by *one* side to replace offensive forces with defensive forces will produce defensive superiority for both, i.e. it will produce mutual defensive superiority. Thus suppose country *A* replaces forces that have a strong offensive capability with forces that have a strong defensive capability, whilst country *B* keeps its forces unchanged. The result will be that *A* has increased its defensive capability above the unchanged offensive capability of B; and at the same time A has reduced its offensive capability below the defensive capability of B.* (See box below.)

The same arguments of course apply if we start from positions other than balanced all-round forces.

If we start from Mutual Offensive Superiority, implying that mutual dissuasion is maintained by mutual threat of retaliation, a transition to Mutual Defensive Superiority may be harder to achieve than if we start from balanced all-round forces because there is a risk, in theory at least, that as the transition from Mutual Offensive Superiority is made, one side may find itself enjoying both offensive superiority and defensive superiority, i.e. 'all-round' superiority, so that it has its opponent at its mercy. This will happen if that side increases its defensive strength too fast and reduces its offensive strength too slowly in relation to the changes made by its opponent. It is also true that, starting from balanced all-round forces, all-round superiority will be achieved by one side if it simply increases forces or adds to their offensive capability keeping their defensive capability constant. But that is another way of saying that balanced all-round forces are unstable because either side can so easily achieve superiority – in theory at least.

---

*The starting position is

$$D_A = O_A = D_B = O_B.$$

Country A increases its defensive forces D_A and reduces its offensive forces O_A, while country B keeps D_B and O_B constant. We then have $D_A > O_B$ and $D_B > O_B$, which is Mutual Defensive Superiority.

The alternative way of achieving Mutual Defensive Superiority is for both sides to reduce their offensive forces starting from:

$$D_A = O_A = D_B = O_B$$

Reductions in O_A and O_B, whilst D_A and D_B are held constant, produce

$$D_A > O_B, D_B > O_A$$

THE MORE-THAN-TWO COUNTRY PROBLEM

So far we have considered the alternative strategies open to *two* countries with a common frontier which arm against each other but do not both have nuclear weapons. We have ignored the existence of more than two countries.

The two country analysis can be applied to two geographically united alliances with a common frontier, if those alliances are sufficiently homogeneous to have a common strategy. For in that event two alliances are, for the purposes of analysing alternative strategies, no different from two countries. Or, to put it more generally, a geographically united alliance with a single strategy is equivalent to a country, and all our propositions about countries apply to homogeneous alliances.

As the number of countries (or alliances) increases, the harder it is for each to achieve Mutual Defensive Superiority *vis-à-vis* its neighbours, assuming each has to be prepared for the possibiity that the others may combine against it. Since the forces chosen for defensive capability will still have some offensive capability, the forces that country A needs to achieve defensive superiority over the combined forces of B and C may, for example, have offensive superiority over B alone and perhaps C alone. If so, Mutual Defensive Superiority, and hence stability, cannot be achieved. For this reason, the larger the number of independent countries (i.e. countries that are not firmly allied) the greater the potential military instability in their mutual relations. Europe before 1914 is an example (see Appendix).

But that is not all. A more severe form of instability can occur when there is one strong country in the middle. It is a problem that manifested itself in relations between Germany and its neighbours before 1914 and in the inter-war period. Before 1914, Germany had become powerful and was feared by France to her West and by Russia to her East. Since France and Russia each doubted its ability to defend itself alone against Germany, they agreed to join forces against Germany if either of them was attacked by her. This meant that each needed offensive forces capable of attacking quickly, so that if Germany attacked France, Russia could quickly attack Germany in the East and help France by drawing forces away from the western front; and if Germany attacked Russia, France could quickly attack Germany and draw forces away from the eastern front.

How the Germans saw the problem was explained by Schlieffen:

Germany has the advantage of lying between France and Russia and of separating these allies. It would lose this advantage if it were to divide its army and thus be inferior in numbers to each single opponent. Germany must strive, therefore, first, to strike down one of the allies while the other is kept occupied; but then, when the one antagonist is conquered, it must, by exploiting its railways, bring a superiority of numbers to the other theatre of war, which will also destroy the other enemy. The first blow must be delivered with the utmost power and a really decisive battle must take place.[7]

In general terms, the conditions that give rise to this particular need for offensive forces are these:

(a) There is a strong central power.
(b) That central power has offensive forces.
(c) The central power has two (or more) neighbours who, because of geographical separation, cannot in the event of war hope to reinforce each other's forces by sending expeditionary forces fast enough to be able to save each other from being overwhelmed by an attack by the undivided strength of the central power.
(d) The two (or more) neighbours can hope to avoid or resist attack by the central power if, by threat of attack, they can keep the forces of the central power divided.

There are various possible solutions to this problem – if intentions are peaceful:

(a) The central power and its two neighbours can adopt defensive strategies in concert with one another.
(b) The central power can take the initiative and adopt a defensive strategy on its own, if the effectiveness of the defence it can mount is such that it can expect to hold off both neighbours by that means.
(c) It may be possible for the nations to be formed into alliances with other powers so that a more stable pattern is formed.

NUCLEAR WEAPONS ON ONE SIDE

If – and here we resume the two-country model – one side possesses nuclear weapons, the basic conditions of the classical setting still hold for reasons we noted earlier. The nation that possesses nuclear weapons can use those weapons to threaten attack and, if need be, to attack, without fear of retaliation.

If the intentions of the nuclear power are peaceful towards its non-nuclear neighbour, it can seek to reassure its neighbour and achieve stability by going for Mutual Defensive Superiority in non-nuclear forces, geography and technology permitting, and perhaps by being as unprovocative as possible with its nuclear weapons.

If the aims of the nuclear power are offensive, a narrow military calculus would suggest that it could threaten to attack its neighbour with nuclear weapons, reckoning that its nuclear forces gave it overall military superiority, regardless of its relative strength at the non-nuclear level. But to calculate that you can be more destructive than your neighbour is no guide as to whether it will pay you politically to attack him. That will depend on the political odium you would incur if you made a nuclear attack and on the politico–economic gain (or liability) that would accrue to you in the shape of the shattered country you had attacked (Chapter 3).

THE NUCLEAR SETTING

In a nuclear setting where two sides possess nuclear weapons sufficient to do each other unacceptable damage, there are two coherent policies that might be followed. These are polar opposites. There has been a vain search for intermediate policies, which is examined in Chapter 3.

The first policy is to seek to maintain the nuclear setting, on the grounds that you need some nuclear weapons to prevent your neighbour threatening to attack you, or attacking you, with nuclear weapons, though you recognise that because he too has nuclear weapons you are constrained from taking the initiative in using them by the risk of retaliation.

The second policy is to seek to break out of the nuclear setting by acquiring the means to neutralise your opponent's nuclear forces.

A third policy, which can be regarded as an extension of the first policy, is to seek to down-grade, limit or remove nuclear weapons by negotiation or by changes in strategy.

With the first policy, your strategy is to dissuade your opponent from nuclear attack by threat of retaliation; the appropriate military stance is to have enough nuclear weapons to be able to do unaccept-able damage to your opponent after allowing for failures and for losses he may inflict on your nuclear forces. We shall call this stance *Sufficiency*. And we can write

$$S = X + M$$

where S stands for sufficiency, X for the number of weapons you think you need in order to do unacceptable damage to your enemy, and M stands for the margin of extra weapons you need in order to allow for failures and losses. The value of M will be influenced by the number of weapons possessed by your opponent insofar as his weapons have the capacity to inflict losses on yours. That will depend upon the characteristics of his weapons – on whether he goes for a first strike capability or for an invulnerable second strike capability; and whether he goes for defences or not. The value of X should be independent of the size of your opponent's forces. There is no point in acquiring the capability to do unacceptable damage to his popula-tion several times over, even if he wastes his energies acquiring the capability to do that to your population.

With the second policy – to try to break out of the nuclear setting – you wish to be free to attack – or make uninhibited threats of attack with nuclear weapons. The military stance you require is that you should be able to inflict such losses on your opponent's nuclear forces, by means of pre-emptive strikes or defences, that he cannot do unacceptable damage to you. This means returning to a position that approximates to a monopoly of nuclear weapons. We shall call it *Supremacy*. The chances of success with this policy are likely to be small, not to say negligible, since your opponent is likely to produce counter-measures to any measures you introduce; and you can never know how your weapons and his will work unless you have a nuclear exchange. Moreover the uncertainty whether you can derive much political advantage from one-sided use, or threat of use, of nuclear weapons must not be forgotten. But, feasibility and political reality aside, logic dictates that Supremacy, as defined here, is the nuclear stance to pursue if you wish to break free of the constraints that a nuclear stalemate impose on you.

If you are pursuing Sufficiency, the force structure you will seek will be an invulnerable second strike capability. If you are pursuing Supremacy, you will pursue a first strike capability, possibly combined with defences against your opponent's nuclear weapons.

Just as your opponent will infer your intentions at the non-nuclear level from what he sees of your non-nuclear force structure, as well as from what you say about your political aims and strategy, so he will infer your intentions at the nuclear level from your nuclear force structure and from what you say – or refrain from saying – about your political aims and nuclear strategy. The alternatives are illustrated in Figure 2.2.

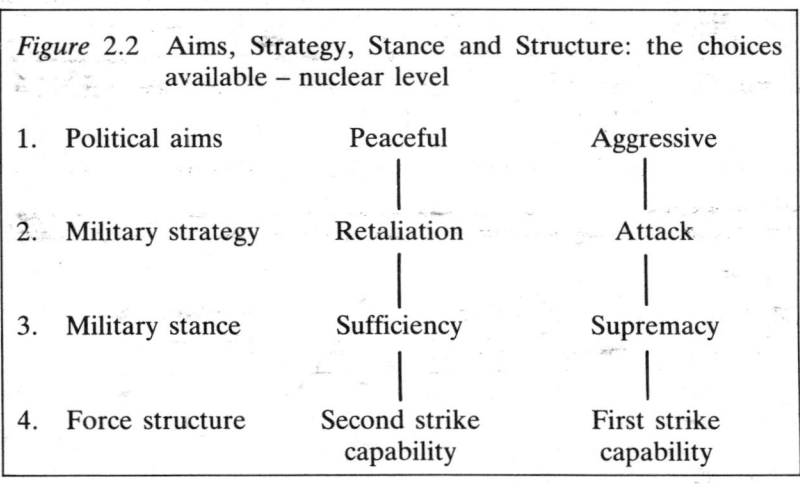

Figure 2.2 Aims, Strategy, Stance and Structure: the choices available – nuclear level

1.	Political aims	Peaceful	Aggressive
2.	Military strategy	Retaliation	Attack
3.	Military stance	Sufficiency	Supremacy
4.	Force structure	Second strike capability	First strike capability

In a nuclear setting the adoption of Sufficiency and a second strike capability is the most reassuring signal that you can send to your opponent. The introduction of defences, meaning systems that will impede the nuclear weapons of your opponent, is a move that will alarm rather than reassure your opponent, since it is a move that suggests you are seeking to limit his power to retaliate and in so doing are aiming for Supremacy.

BALANCE AND NUCLEAR WEAPONS

With nuclear weapons, as with non-nuclear weapons, it can readily be seen that the pursuit of balance, meaning equality in numbers of weapons, is a policy that makes no sense.

If your aims are peaceful, Sufficiency is the objective to pursue at the nuclear level and it makes no sense to go beyond it. If your aims are offensive, balance is a wholly inadequate objective. Your objective, though unattainable, must be Supremacy. If you seek to be adventurous at the non-nuclear level whilst in a nuclear stalemate, there is no point in going beyond Sufficiency and pursuing balance or superiority.

Although it is obvious that there is a saturation point and that above Sufficiency relative numbers of nuclear weapons have no military significance (short of unattainable Supremacy), it is frequently said or implied that there is political value in relative strength in nuclear weapons at levels above Sufficiency. Failure to keep up in the pursuit of balance is seen as lack of resolution, even as a sign that you lack the political will to use nuclear weapons. Nuclear weapons are seen almost as status symbols: we cannot let them have more than we have. There is belief in the psychological effects of nuclear superiority and nuclear inferiority (Chapter 6).

CONCLUSION

The burden of the analysis so far is that in a classical setting there are alternative strategies appropriate to different political aims; in a nuclear setting political aims are constrained and the overriding purpose becomes the avoidance of war.

In a nuclear setting, it is the *combination* of your nuclear and non-nuclear strategies – and the stances and force structures that go with those strategies – that matters. Mutual Defensive Superiority at the non-nuclear level and Sufficiency at the nuclear level is the combination that will maximise stability and generate positive feedback by indicating to your neighbour you have minimised your capacity to attack him whilst preserving your security.

3 The Nuclear Level

As was remarked earlier, if only one of two countries has nuclear weapons it can, from a military point of view, make nuclear threats against the other, and execute those threats, with the same freedom as it can make, and execute, threats to use conventional forces. In this respect it is in a classical setting. Nuclear threats of this kind have been called, misleadingly, nuclear blackmail, and the argument that you need nuclear weapons in order to avoid nuclear blackmail has been used by nuclear powers, for example Britain, to justify their possession of nuclear weapons. Yet nuclear blackmail has also been dismissed, implicitly, or explicitly, by nuclear powers when they advocate non-proliferation and argue that nations that do not yet possess nuclear weapons do not need them. There has been more opportunism than consistency in the way the notion of 'nuclear blackmail' has been used.

The judgement whether it is advantageous to make a nuclear threat will not depend on a military calculus, meaning an expert estimate whether your forces are stronger than those of the other side and will win. For if you alone have nuclear weapons, your forces are incomparably the stronger in destructive power. That being so, you must turn to political rather than military considerations in order to judge whether it will be to your advantage either to make a nuclear threat or to use nuclear weapons.[1]

To make that political judgement, the political leaders of the nuclear power will have to assess the political reactions of the opponent, of the rest of the world and of the political community at home. They will have to ask themselves whether the other side is likely to yield to whatever political demand is being made of them. Are they likely to surrender, as the Japanese did when they were in any case near to defeat and enjoyed little political sympathy in the world? Or are they likely to resist and appeal to world opinion? And how is foreign opinion, and opinion in the country making the threat, likely to react? It is political considerations of this kind that will be decisive.

That nuclear threats have been rare and that nuclear weapons have never been used since 1945 suggests that the political inhibitions have been strong. But it should not be assumed that the political inhibitions are fixed and cannot be broken down – or reinforced.

29

Moreover, threats have mostly been made between the Soviet Union and the United States, both of which are nuclear powers, *not* by nuclear powers against non-nuclear powers, even when they have faced defeat, for example the United States in Vietnam and the Soviet Union in Afghanistan.

When there is a nuclear setting, i.e. when two nations possess nuclear weapons with the assured capacity to annihilate each other, force is excessive on both sides; neither side can be stronger than the other; there can be no expectation of victory based on a military calculus of relative strength.

The survival of your society, which must be your first priority, is at risk and depends on the restraint of your neighbour. The fate of you and your neighbour is bound together: if either of you attacks the other, he risks suffering retaliation, fall-out that is blown back onto him and possibly a nuclear winter or other unforeseen consequence of nuclear war.

As we saw in Chapter 2, there are two polar courses of action that can be followed. We now examine these more closely.

THE ACCEPTANCE OF STALEMATE AND ITS IMPLICATIONS

The first policy is to accept that there is a stalemate, that the only reason (if it is one) for keeping nuclear weapons is to avoid being threatened or attacked by those who possess them. In this case the rational force posture is nuclear Sufficiency, as we defined it earlier, achieved by the possession of invulnerable second strike forces. The implication of this stance is that you accept that, at least in a nuclear setting, nuclear weapons have no military, war-fighting use. You seek only nuclear-to-nuclear deterrence; you seek to reassure your neighbour and to seek a political solution to any disputes. The corollary at the non-nuclear level of the pursuit of nuclear Sufficiency is the pursuit of Mutual Defensive Superiority so as to produce stability and positive feedback. The risk of nuclear war depends on the stability and feed-back characteristics of *both* non-nuclear and nuclear forces. A nuclear war may start at either level.

Whether nuclear weapons can serve the purpose of nuclear-to-nuclear deterrence only is a difficult question to answer. It is sometimes suggested that the existence of nuclear weapons or even the knowledge of how to make them will cause 'existential deterrence', meaning caution in the resort to war. The implication is that the effect of weapons held for nuclear-to-nuclear deterrence will overflow and provide some deterrence to challenges at the non-nuclear level; or that after nuclear disarmament, if it was achieved, the memory of nuclear weapons might cause continuing political restraint.[2]

These notions are rather nebulous. To try and see what meaning one can give to them, we can start from the proposition that if your neighbour possesses nuclear weapons, there is a probability, however small, that he would use them if you made demands on him or attacked him with non-nuclear weapons; and that probability will in some degree deter you from those actions.

Against this it can be argued that the existence of a weapon does not generate deterrence. There must be a belief that the weapon might be used. Take the example of knives and forks. These are lethal instruments. At any meal anyone could use them mortally to injure whoever is sitting next to him. But we do not entertain the idea of using knives and forks like that, nor do we keep our knives or forks in readiness so as to deter whoever is eating with us from attacking us. Society has become civilised to the point where such behaviour has been left behind. The attempts to outlaw chemical weapons can be regarded as attempts to move from a world where the possession of these weapons by one nation deters their use by others to a world where their possession is outlawed by treaty, followed, ideally, by an eventual transition to a world where, by custom, the use of chemical weapons, like the aggressive use of knives and forks, is simply not contemplated. One can conceive of the same evolution for nuclear weapons. In that optimistic perspective, existential deterrence, meaning that people are knowingly restrained by the threat of nuclear war, would be a transitional condition prior to the condition, if it ever came about, when peace was assured by other means and people ceased to think about nuclear weapons as a threat: when the number of weapons needed for nuclear Sufficiency was zero.

For movement towards that condition to be made possible whilst security is preserved, it would be necessary to stop competing in nuclear weapons and reduce their level to a minimum, as part of a process of seeking reconciliation with nuclear rivals; and it would be advisable to stop uttering nuclear threats and pointing nuclear weapons at particular nations and shift to the position that nuclear weapons are in reserve, ready to be used against anyone in the last resort; they are there as a quiet reminder that we live in a nuclear setting in which caution is appropriate: if there is a war the risk of nuclear war cannot be excluded.[3]

Whether nuclear arsenals could eventually be reduced to zero rather than some smaller number is a question that may seem rather academic now when the nuclear arsenals of the leading powers are so vast, but it is a question that merits some attention since it is sometimes argued that because nuclear weapons cannot be 'disinvented' or because the other side might cheat and retain a weapon or two, no nuclear nation could risk going to zero; and on these grounds it has sometimes been argued that it is not sensible to embark on any substantial degree of nuclear disarmament. That does not follow. It may be very sensible to reduce nuclear arsenals in a process of reconciliation, even if you do not go to zero. But what does it mean to say that you cannot go to zero? And what is the meaning of cheating?

If each of a group of nations that have renounced nuclear weapons has once possessed them and has nuclear power plants, each will have the physical capability to produce a nuclear weapon, after an interval of greater or lesser length, if it wishes to threaten or attack another nation, or if there is a need to retaliate or threaten retaliation against a nation that becomes excessively threatening. As in the case of knives and forks, instruments will be available, perhaps after an interval, which can be used lethally, even if lethal use, and the explicit threat of it, has ceased to be customary. Hence if by formal nuclear disarmament you scrapped all nuclear warheads and the delivery systems that go with them, you would reach zero in terms of ready-made weapons but not in terms of potential weapons that could be made. Whether and when it would be wise formally to scrap all existing nuclear weapons by agreement would depend on the political setting and the security arrangements that had been achieved and were in prospect. It cannot be said without regard to the setting that it is a step that can or cannot be taken.

The argument that you cannot go to zero nuclear weapons because of the risk of cheating rests on the reasonable proposition that no one could ever verify with 100 per cent certainty that no nuclear weapon existed, in combination with the questionable assumption that if one nation cheated it could make a significant political gain by making a nuclear threat or nuclear attack. We have already seen that the achievement of a political gain by making a nuclear threat ('nuclear blackmail') is problematical when the threatener possesses nuclear weapons and *knows* that his victim does not possess them. If the threatener has cheated in a disarmament treaty he faces a more complex problem. He must recognise that his victim may have cheated too or, more precisely, he must recognise that he can never be certain that his victim has not cheated. Hence in response to his threat and his accompanying admission (or claim) that he has cheated, his victim might say, 'Look out, I have cheated too'. The threatener would then be in a dilemma. He could not be sure it was not so. And in any case his victim, as an ex-nuclear power, would possess the ability to produce a weapon with greater or lesser delay. Hence in the scenario of one ex-nuclear power cheating and threatening another, the risk of retaliation can never be wholly absent.

In sum, the proposition that you cannot know for certain if your neighbour has gone to zero does not constitute a case against embarking on nuclear disarmament, nor even does it necessarily constitute a case against going eventually to zero.

THE PURSUIT OF POLITICAL ADVANTAGE

The second policy that can be adopted in a nuclear setting is to reject the notion of stalemate and seek political gain. If that aim is adopted, the method of achieving it that makes theoretical sense is, as we have seen, to try to break out of the nuclear setting by introducing defences and first strike weapons until you achieve Supremacy, i.e. a position where you are ready to sustain such reduced damage as your opponent could do to you and could still inflict unacceptable damage on him. For reasons explained in Chapter 2, that is an aim that does not look remotely attainable. And it is a policy which will maximise instability and negative feedback.

The alternative is to try, without Supremacy, i.e. while still in a nuclear setting, actively to use the possession of nuclear weapons for purposes additional to nuclear-to-nuclear deterrence. We have seen that the fact that you possess at least a Sufficiency of nuclear weapons may induce some caution in your neighbour as regards his conduct at the sub-nuclear level even if you declare that your reason for keeping your nuclear weapons is nuclear-to-nuclear deterrence only.

The questions that have to be faced are whether, and how, in these circumstances you can intensify that threat to your opponent? And can you do it without increasing the threat to yourself equally?

The answer in brief is that – assuming always that you are in a nuclear setting – any action you take that increases the threat to your opponent will increase the 'shared risk', i.e. the risk common to yourself and your opponent, that nuclear weapons will be used. The idea that you might be able to twist the risk, so that the risk to your opponent is increased more than the risk to yourself, has been explored frequently – and fruitlessly. The reasons for this we shall now examine.

NUCLEAR WEAPONS ONLY

We shall start by considering two neighbouring countries that possess nuclear weapons *only*. We shall assume that each has sufficient invulnerable nuclear weapons to be able to annihilate the other: we are in a nuclear setting with no non-nuclear weapons.

We shall make the strong, worst-case assumptions, common to most reasoning about nuclear strategy, that the other side is relentlessly hostile and so are you; that you seek to intimidate him so as to stop him from seeking to make gains, often of an unspecified nature, by challenging and testing your will to retaliate; and you seek to make gains from him.

Suppose first that each side could only use all its nuclear weapons or none: it could not go in for gradual escalation – an assumption which, though made for purposes of simplification, is not wholly unrealistic, since it is uncertain whether the use of nuclear weapons could or would be controlled and gradual, once it started.

The first aim will be to avoid the use of nuclear weapons, since the avoidance of annihilation must be your first priority. Self-deterrence operates, as well as the deterrence of your neighbour; the risk of annihilation is shared and, since you will value your survival more highly than that of your neighbour, self-deterrence should be the dominant consideration.

In this setting the political aims of both sides will be constrained. But suppose there is an issue, for example, a frontier dispute, that you cannot settle to your satisfaction by political means; you therefore start considering if you can achieve results by threatening to use your nuclear weapons.

You will find that it is impossible to say how to make a nuclear threat in such a way as to make your neighbour yield. For you know that he, who is in the same situation as you, knows that you are self-deterred and do not wish to annihilate yourself along with him. Your threat can only be a bluff, a try-on. Any loud and alarming noises and gestures you make cannot be relied upon to get you out of the stalemate, for they can be interpreted either as a sign of weakness

– that you dare only to make a noise – or as a sign of strength – that you are ready to act. Similarly a silent, calm stance can be interpreted as a sign of strength or a sign of weakness.

Sometimes a threat may work, but that does not alter the fact that there are no objective means of knowing whether or when threats will work; nor if you succeed once, do you have any grounds for expecting to succeed again. In a nuclear setting, strategy, meaning the use of superior force, or the use of threats that you will use superior force so as to make your opponent yield to your wishes, collapses because there is saturation of force: neither side can be stronger than the other; therefore neither side can say that this or that use of force is a winning move, nor make a threat that is backed by a winning move. Any threat is a complete gamble.

GAME THEORY

A way out of this impasse was sought in game theory, but the theory has proved to be inapplicable; it has never been used in nuclear targeting or policy-making; at most, it has provided some analogies and has perhaps helped to convey the point that, in a nuclear setting, strategy, meaning the calculus of how to use force, collapses through saturation of force, leaving you with nothing but fear and bluff.

The reason game theory is inapplicable is that a game requires rules, meaning that it is laid down in advance that specified actions by you and responses by your opponent will lead to outcomes with a pre-determined pay-off, i.e. a win or loss of so much. In a nuclear setting, where there is saturation of force, the only rule is that, if you make any move, you may be annihilated. It is as if you were offered a game of chess in which both players started in checkmate and all possible moves left them both in checkmate – or both dead. There is no game.[4]

The principal analogy to the problems of policy in a nuclear setting was the game of chicken, supposedly played by teenagers to test their bravado.[5] Two people in cars drive at each other head on and the loser is the driver who swerves first to avoid collision. A typical question was, could a player improve his chances of winning by feigning to be drunk? Or by detaching and throwing away his steering wheel in a manner visible to his opponent? These are not moves in a game. The first is a way of bluffing, the second a way of adding physically to the shared risks.

ESCALATION

We now drop the assumption that the two countries can only use all their nuclear weapons or none, and consider nuclear escalation.

The idea is to threaten your opponent with the prospect of an all-out nuclear exchange not just by making threats in words but by using nuclear weapons progressively with ascending violence. Associated with this has been the notion that you may be able to achieve 'escalation dominance'.

It is assumed that there is a ladder of steps representing actions of increasing violence that lead upwards to the all-out nuclear exchange which must be avoided at all costs. According to the theory, the steps short of the top of the ladder are not totally unacceptable, though they are increasingly nasty. But it is not their increasing nastiness that matters. It is the fact that they lead to the top, unacceptable step. It is for this reason that your opponent – and you – will be unwilling to be forced up the ladder. And it is that unwillingness in the other that both will try to play on.

The idea of a ladder was first presented by Herman Kahn only 'as a metaphor . . . without trying to make a rigorous analogy', and the ladder he offered, with 44 steps, more than half of them nuclear, was utterly fantastical.[6] But the idea of controlled escalation has persisted.

In order to examine the idea, let us start by assuming that there is a range of targets of increasing value you can hit with nuclear weapons and – a pair of strong assumptions – that the two sides have identical ladders and these can be recognised by both. Suppose you go to step 1 and hit some minor target. Your opponent can retaliate at the same level or go up as many steps as he likes, but what he and you do at any point short of the top step will not be conclusive. He can refrain from retaliation and say that, rather than make any political concessions, he will escalate when he feels like it. If he does so, you will not have won anything for he can always go to the top step or any point short of it that he chooses. *Ex hypothesi*, you both retain the capacity to do unacceptable damage by going to the top step, and the damage done at these lower steps is acceptable. In short, escalation is just a way of threatening, by actions rather than words, that you will go to the top, and it suffers from just the same ambiguity as the making of threats in words. Is a warning shot – a common idea for a first step – a sign of strength (you dare to shoot first) or a sign of weakness (you dare to make only a warning shot)? An excess of nuclear weapons, such as exists now, does not increase the length of the theoretical ladder. For the length depends on the number of discrete steps that can be identified in terms of type of target and the intensity of attack, and upon how much damage you are prepared to accept before you decide it is unacceptable: if the use of one nuclear weapon is unacceptable, there is no ladder to play on.

A closer examination of the idea of escalation reveals more difficulties. What is your scale of targets, starting from those whose loss you value least if your opponent attacks them (which will be at the bottom of the ladder) and going up to those you value most? For example, are airfields more valuable than harbours?

And what is your opponent's scale of values? Suppose he values airfields more highly than harbours and you do the opposite, how are you both to know that? And if you do know it, whose scale of values are you to follow when you escalate? And how are you to know which scale your opponent is following? If you do not know these things, you may reach dangerously wrong conclusions. Your opponent may think you have escalated when you did not intend to do so, or the opposite; and, similarly, you may misinterpret his actions. The point can be illustrated by the story of a western visitor to a middle eastern country who, before going out to visit some local people in the evening, was advised by friends with whom she was staying that etiquette required that, when she was offered dinner, she should refuse three times; she would then be fed. She obeyed instructions, but no meal appeared; she came back hungry. Her friends who had advised her made enquiries and found that her hosts of the evening had assumed that she was following western conventions.[7]

There is the further and most serious difficulty that if you take a single step at the bottom of the ladder, you may provoke all-out retaliation so that your whole notion of playing on the ladder proves calamitously wrong. This may happen for a number of reasons. Your neighbour, swayed by or unable to overcome his military's appetite for using everything they have got and hoping they may knock out your weapons, may have planned all-out retaliation; or through miscalculation, misunderstanding or an over-zealous interpretation of orders, a chain of events may be started that leads to all-out use. Indeed he may seek to keep these risks alive precisely in order to dissuade you from using or threatening to use any nuclear weapons.

Thus we are driven back to the point that you can increase the shared risk of nuclear catastrophe, but in a nuclear setting there is no way of increasing the risk to your opponent more than to yourself and hence obtaining a differential advantage.

RAISING THE RISK

Another approach that has been suggested is to place your opponent in a position where you can persuade him that, if he does not yield to your political demands, he may start an escalatory process of challenges and responses by the two sides in which developments may get out of control and lead, perhaps by miscalculation, misinterpretation or over-zealous interpretation of orders, to the use of nuclear weapons and possibly an all-out nuclear exchange.

One suggested way of producing this challenge has been openly to diminish control over your weapons so as to scare your opponent, in a manner comparable to the notion, noted earlier, of throwing away the steering wheel in the game of chicken. It has been called 'the threat that leaves something to chance'. A practical example is to put your nuclear forces on alert thereby removing some safety catches and perhaps making it visibly hard for you to back down without loss of face. This was done by the United States during the 1973 Middle East crisis.[8] But moves of this kind are just more ways of increasing the shared risk or of bluffing; and they can be played by two.

It has been widely recognised by theorists that in a nuclear setting the only way you can increase the risks of nuclear war to your opponent, for the purposes of dissuading him from attacking you, is to increase the risks to yourself as well. Glenn Snyder coined the phrase 'the stability–instability paradox',[9] meaning that the more stable is the nuclear balance (i.e. the less credible is resort to nuclear weapons) the greater the temptation to use force at a lower level knowing that a nuclear response is unlikely, and *vice versa*. And with reference to the policy of calculatedly increasing the shared risk, Herman Kahn spoke of 'the rationality of the irrational'.[10]

It is important to recognise that these paradoxical statements mean only that one can conceive of persons who thought it was worth raising the risk of mutual annihilation in the belief that they would thereby increase their chance of keeping their neighbours at bay. It does not mean that a policy of increasing instability and negative feedback in this way is in any degree advisable in either its short-run or its long-run consequences.[11] That it is not advisable is one of the arguments used alike by advocates of nuclear Supremacy and by advocates of Sufficiency and restraint.

ESCALATION DOMINANCE

Another possible way of seeking advantage that has been pursued is the idea of 'escalation dominance'. This is the notion that you could derive a relative advantage if you could match or outclass your opponent at each level of violence short of an all-out nuclear exchange, so that you can deny him any military advantage from any moves he may make.[12] This poses several problems.

First, it is a notion that depends on relative strength. Yet with nuclear weapons – or with any terminal weapons – a saturation point may be reached at any or every step on a supposed ladder, after which relative numbers are irrelevant. Indeed that is the very nature of terminal weapons. For example, if attacks on airfields are considered a step on a ladder, both sides may have more than enough nuclear weapons to knock out each other's airfields and still have enough weapons, or more than enough, for all other categories of targets.

Secondly, the notion that it is possible to achieve escalation dominance on a step of a ladder of nuclear weapons rests on the assumption that nuclear weapons are specific to targets, defined by reference to a type of target or an area. For the only way you can define dominance on a step is to say that you have more weapons than he has that are capable of knocking out a given type of target, or a given type of target in a given area. If several types of nuclear weapons have the range and accuracy to knock out targets of a given type, they must all be bundled into one category for the purpose of defining the steps on which you might achieve dominance, and that of course reduces the number of steps, makes saturation more likely and the likelihood of dominance less likely.

Thirdly, there is the difficulty that the pursuit of escalation dominance means that, at each step of the ladder where you seek dominance, you must seek the ability to knock out your opponent's nuclear forces while preserving your own. It thus requires the acquisition of first strike forces and defences; it is a policy of pursuing Supremacy at each step; it maximises instability and negative feedback.

Finally, it is impossible to say whether escalation dominance on a step or steps of a *nuclear* ladder – supposing such a thing to exist – would bring any benefit so long as each side possessed at the top of its ladder the ability to do unacceptable damage to the other. For the taking of steps, as we have noted, is a way of threatening, by actions rather than words, to go to the top and cause unacceptable devastation. It is just another way of conveying the threat. If one side possessed superiority on a step and exercised that superiority by using nuclear weapons at that step, the other side could always counter by using weapons on a higher step. To take a simple case, suppose your neighbour has armed himself only with an invulnerable strategic nuclear force, whilst you possess tactical nuclear weapons as well as a strategic nuclear force, would you feel more free to use, and more free to threaten to use, your tactical nuclear weapons than you would if your opponent possessed tactical weapons? Should your neighbour for this reason acquire tactical nuclear weapons? It is a point that has been argued this way and that, notably in France. No firmly-based answer can be given.

Altogether the idea of finely-graded nuclear escalation does not stand up well to close examination. Where escalation has a meaning that is clear to all sides is at the step from non-nuclear to nuclear weapons. To cross that step, whether in a small or large move, is to run a risk of an all-out nuclear exchange.

NUCLEAR PLUS NON-NUCLEAR WEAPONS

The next step is to relax the assumption that the two nations we are considering are armed only with nuclear weapons.

Following the analysis in Chapter 2, we can classify the alternative stances that can be followed at the non-nuclear level as follows:

(a)　Both sides seek non-nuclear Offensive Superiority, either because their political aims are offensive or because their aims are peaceful but they seek to prevent attack by threat of retaliation. They are of sufficiently equal size for it to be impossible for either of them to be sure that it possesses non-nuclear Offensive Superiority i.e. that it would be successful in attack. Uncertainty clouds the assessments they can make of the chances of achieving surprise and going on to victory. But there is fear of attack which is aggravated by the potential bonus for pre-emptive attack at the non-nuclear level.

(b) One side, being altogether stronger, can be said, with considerable confidence, to enjoy Offensive and Defensive Superiority at the non-nuclear level.

(c) There is Mutual Defensive Superiority between the two sides, meaning that they have peaceful aims, have gone for defensive superiority through some combination of independent and joint acts and, being of not dissimilar size, have been able symmetrically to diminish the probability of successful attack to a level where fear of attack is slight.

(d) One side seeks Offensive Superiority, the other Defensive Superiority.

The implications for nuclear strategy of these four positions are these:

(a) Where either side might succeed in a non-nuclear surprise attack and there is pressure to attack pre-emptively, or at least to react quickly in a crisis, there is instability and negative feedback. The risk of non-nuclear war, and hence of escalation to nuclear war, is not minimised. Moreover the knowledge that the other side might succeed in a surprise attack will increase reliance on nuclear weapons in order to discourage any such move: steps may be taken by each side to emphasise, by word and by the acquisition of more threatening nuclear weapons, that nuclear weapons might be used, with the result that the shared risk of their use is in some degree amplified, not minimised. Thus instability at the non-nuclear level may produce instability at the nuclear level too.

(b) If in a nuclear setting one side enjoys all-round non-nuclear superiority, the weaker side may rely on its nuclear weapons to redress the position. To do this it may be tempted to increase the shared risk that nuclear weapons might be used in the event of non-nuclear war. But at the non-nuclear level the position may be more stable than in the previous case because the fear of pre-emptive non-nuclear attack will not be mutual.

(c) Where the two sides follow strategies of Mutual Defensive Superiority, stability will be maximised and feedback positive, two conditions that should minimise the probability of non-nuclear war breaking out and escalating to the use of nuclear weapons. And if reliance on nuclear weapons is minimised there will not be pressure to acquire nuclear weapons in pursuit of the most menacing postures; reliance on nuclear weapons, and the shared risk that they might be used, will be minimised.

(d)　Where one side pursues Offensive Superiority the other Defensive Superiority, the outcome is indeterminate and moderately unstable unless the relative size of their forces dictates that one dominates the other.

Thus sub-nuclear strategy (meaning strategy for the use of non-nuclear forces when nuclear forces are present) influences the risk of war (which is not likely to start at the nuclear level) and the degree of reliance on nuclear weapons. In these ways, non-nuclear strategy is probably the dominant determinant of the magnitude of the 'shared risk' of nuclear war borne by the two sides.

The other main influence on the shared risk of nuclear war is the systemic stability of the nuclear forces themselves. This depends essentially on the invulnerability of nuclear weapons systems and their command and control systems, relative to the kill capability of the weapons that might be used to strike at them; and that in turn depends principally on how far the technical possibilities of producing systems which can be used for a first strike are exploited, either blindly or on the basis of the kind of arguments for relative strength we have been considering. Systemic instability is assumed away in our concept of Sufficiency where we assume that systems are invulnerable and that the pursuit of relative strength is eschewed.

EXTENDED DETERRENCE

The credibility of using nuclear weapons in a nuclear setting to offset non-nuclear inferiority has been questioned on the grounds that it is not credible that a nation would risk a nuclear holocaust for the sake of a lesser objective than the avoidance of a holocaust. It is an argument that rests on the notion, which cannot be dismissed, that the response to a threat should be in some degree proportional to what is at stake. For example, proportionality implies that, if in a nuclear setting one side feared that it would suffer genocide if it lost a war at the non-nuclear level, it would be more likely to risk using nuclear weapons against its opponent than if it foresaw a less awful outcome in the event of sub-nuclear defeat. The more closely the outcome feared by a nation resembles a nuclear holocaust the more credible it is that it would threaten to use nuclear weapons to try to avoid that outcome, on the grounds that, since there is little difference between the two outcomes, there is little to lose if the nuclear threat fails and both outcomes will be avoided if it succeeds. (Israel and South Africa, who feel that their claims to their territory and their right to exist are challenged, come to mind as two countries which, if their neighbours were armed with nuclear weapons, might fear genocide and take this position.)

The argument that it is not credible to rely on nuclear weapons to offset non-nuclear inferiority has been made in criticism of NATO's doctrine of 'first use'.[13] But in this instance doubts about credibility arise for an additional reason, namely that NATO's present doctrine relies on 'extended deterrence', meaning that a nuclear country promises that it will protect a non-nuclear ally by being ready to use nuclear weapons against a potentially hostile nuclear nation if it attacks that ally.

Extended deterrence poses two problems. The first, which is fundamental but simple, is credibility. Can you expect a nation to risk suicide for the sake of an ally? The answer must be that it is less likely to use nuclear weapons for an ally than for itself.

The second, which illustrates the logical vacuum we enter once we are in a nuclear setting, is the problem of how to deploy nuclear weapons in such a way as to make an extended nuclear threat as credible as possible. It is the problem of 'coupling'. It has been discussed mostly with reference to the deployment of United States nuclear weapons in Europe. It is convenient to discuss it in that way here.

NATO's declared doctrine is that if the WTO attacks with non-nuclear forces, it will be met by NATO's non-nuclear forces. If these begin to be overwhelmed, NATO will escalate to the use of tactical nuclear weapons in or around Europe. If the Soviet Union responds by use of nuclear weapons too, the United States will eventually use its strategic nuclear arsenal. In short, NATO doctrine is based on the notion of a ladder with an all-out nuclear exchange at the top, a ladder that has its foot in Europe and its top in the United States.

The argument is over whether it is better to have lots of United States nuclear weapons of different kinds in Europe relative to the Soviet Union, or to have few and rely on the United States strategic arsenal, which is mostly based in the United States or under the seas.

One line of thinking says you must have strong American tactical nuclear forces in Europe compared with the Russians or the threat to use the weapons will not be credible: if the American nuclear forces in Europe are weak, it will appear that the Americans are unlikely to start using nuclear weapons because if they did, they might soon be driven to use their strategic nuclear forces, thereby putting their homeland at risk. The Soviets, seeing this, will be more likely to attack or threaten Western Europe than they would be if the American nuclear forces were stronger. In the jargon, American nuclear weakness in Europe causes nuclear 'decoupling' of America from Europe.

Another line of thinking says, on the contrary, that if in order to restore the coupling, you strengthen American nuclear forces in Europe relative to those of the Russians, the Americans may be more willing to use those forces in Europe precisely because there will be less probability that they will have to go to the top of the ladder and put the United States, rather than Europe, at risk; and the Russians, seeing what has happened, will be more likely to attack Western Europe.

So we are faced by the paradox that what is coupling by one argument is decoupling by the other, and we have no way of choosing between the two arguments. We are left in the impasse that what couples decouples; and what decouples couples – an example of the logical incoherence of deterrence theory.

MORE THAN TWO COUNTRIES

So far we have followed the mainstream of nuclear strategy in assuming that there are two countries only. It is a simplifying assumption that greatly facilitates analysis. It should be noted however that it has the unintended effect of reinforcing the notion that there are only two nuclear powers that matter, which carries with it the false implication that the nuclear arsenals of the other nuclear nations are negligible.

As the possession of nuclear weapons spreads to more areas, nuclear caution may spread. On the other hand, the theoretical problems of stability become greater in a mechanical way as the number of nuclear nations within range of one another increases. It is harder to achieve Sufficiency if you do not know how many other nations might combine against you and try to knock out your nuclear forces: if each nation tries to be sure it has enough, it may be that none can reach his target. The result, theoretically at least, will be pressure to attack pre-emptively in a time of crisis and also upward feedback as the nations compete to get enough weapons.

Similarly, the greater the number of nuclear powers the harder it will be, if nuclear weapons are ever used, to know who is firing them at whom and how to retaliate, if at all.

Beyond these mechanical effects of the spread of nuclear weapons, which may be offset or accentuated by the tide of political sentiment towards nuclear weapons and by changes in the climate of international relations, one cannot say much, except that there are no grounds for supposing that those who acquire nuclear weapons late will be more or less responsible than those who have acquired them early.

CONCLUSION

So long as two nations are in a nuclear setting, there is no way that one can threaten to attack, or expect to be able to make a nuclear attack against the other, without incurring, via the threat of retaliation, an equal risk to itself. Nor is it realistic for them to hope to break out of the nuclear setting by attempting to achieve Supremacy. A nuclear stalemate is a nuclear stalemate. Upon examination, the tricks suggested for making threats successfully in a nuclear setting can be seen to be bluff or moves that will raise the risk shared by both sides, not just the risk to the victim of the threat.

To pursue peaceful aims, the appropriate stance with nuclear forces, which are inherently offensive and threatening, is nuclear Sufficiency. But the principal way to reduce the risk of nuclear war is through non-nuclear strategy. It is at the non-nuclear level that war is most likely to start; and it is at the non-nuclear level that there is some choice between an offensive and a defensive stance and force structure.

4 The Sub-Nuclear Level

This chapter considers the principles on which forces should be constructed in order to achieve Defensive Superiority, and the problems of achieving that stance. We shall consider a nuclear setting, i.e. a setting where the possibility of resort to nuclear weapons by either side must be taken into account. Most of what is said is applicable, however, to a non-nuclear setting.

ORIGINS

The idea that, in a nuclear setting, non-nuclear strategy and non-nuclear forces should be defensive was put forward, and explored with his usual brilliance, by Sir Basil Liddell Hart in his book, *Deterrent or Defence*, in 1960. Liddell Hart argued that, in a nuclear setting, 'To aim at winning a war, to take victory as your object, is no more than a state of lunacy', and he advocated a 'non-nuclear fireguard and fire-extinguisher'.[1] As West Germany was being rearmed, a West German officer, Bogislav von Bonin, had argued that the strategy and force structure of the new Bundeswehr was too offensive and should be made defensive, with reliance on a wide belt of passive infantry and prepared defences that could not be perceived as a threat.[2] Later a French officer, Guy Brossollet, in his seminal *Essai sur la Non-Bataille* published in 1975, carried a similar line of thinking further and argued, contrary to all the military traditions which have grown up in a classical setting, that strategy must aim to avoid a decisive battle, to avoid a quick decision in favour of one side or the other.[3] A further contribution came at about the same time from an Austrian officer, E. Spannocchi, in an essay on defence without self-destruction.[4]

A number of models of defensive defence were then developed in West Germany. The purest – because it pursued the logic of defensiveness to the limits without compromise – was that of Horst Afheldt.[5] In his model, total reliance was placed on dispersed forces capable of long-range and short-range fire, using precision-guided

46

munitions to provide, across the whole area to be defended, a network in which an attacker would meet endless resistance coming from forces which, owing to their dispersal, he could not detect and attack in rewarding numbers. No mobile armoured forces, capable of attack or counter-attack, were included. The prospect of endless resistance in a war of attrition was relied upon to dissuade the potential enemy from attack.

The models subsequently produced by others in Germany generally have combined a network of this kind in an area behind the frontier with mobile forces in the rear for the purpose of stopping attacking forces that make headway and driving them back. The main variation amongst the models is in the quantity of mobile forces relative to networks and in the types of new 'high-tech' weapon used in the network, for example, anti-tank weapons, pre-positioned or projected mines, smart missiles and advanced sensors.[6]

All this work has dealt until recently with the pursuit of nonnuclear defensive superiority by one side on the assumption that the other side retains all-round forces or forces designed to take the offensive. This 'one-sided' case is the toughest test of a strategy of defensive defence: it is much easier to show that security will be enhanced in the 'two-sided' case, where both sides reduce their offensive capabilities together. We shall consider the two-sided case later.

There have been two reasons for the concentration on the onesided case. In the first place, the work was done in Western Europe at a time when it did not seem at all plausible that the Soviet Union and Warsaw Pact would entertain the idea of defensive defence, let alone take the initiative and propose it to NATO, as they have done recently. Study was therefore devoted to the one-sided adoption of defensive defence by NATO.

The second reason is that, even where the eventual aim is to consider the two-sided case, it is necessary first to explore whether and how one side can on its own change the structure of its forces so as to increase its defensive capability and reduce its offensive capability *vis-à-vis* an opponent who does not follow suit. It is the best way of seeing the possibilities and the difficulties of making strategy and force structures defensive. For the same reason we shall start by analysing the one-sided case.

Before proceeding, it is useful to look briefly at the main trends in the technology of weapons and firepower, and their possible implications for defence and offense.

THE TREND OF TECHNOLOGY AND FIREPOWER

It is possible to discern in the history of industrial development three main waves of technological innovation that have taken place over the past 100 years or so. Each has been applied to the production of armaments.[7]

First there was the era of the engineering, ship-building and chemical industries. This saw the development and production of breach-loading artillery and machine guns, and ammunition for them, on such a scale that land warfare became a competition in the application of massed firepower by massed armies of low mobility. The First World War was the climax of that era. Static firepower put the defence in the ascendant.[8] No one could break through the massed fire of machine guns deployed in trenches defended by barbed wire. The cavalry, the old instrument of mobile warfare, was finished, and so was the foot soldier advancing with a bayonet.

Next came the era of the automobile and aircraft industries, the era of the internal combustion engine. The application of the technologies of this era began in the First World War. Tanks were then used, albeit hesitantly, to wade through and suppress enemy machine gun fire while infantry followed on foot. Aircraft were used for reconnaissance and for bombardment, though the scale of aerial bombardment was trivial by modern standards. The ascendancy of the defence was challenged, and that was the beginning, the seed from which was born the practice of mobile warfare which dominated military thinking and practice in the Second World War and has continued to dominate military thinking since then. The architects of mobile warfare, notably Fuller and Liddell Hart, saw the possibility of using tanks not as aids to the infantry that moved at walking pace in the context of a static war but as the modern equivalent of cavalry. Infantry should be put into vehicles which, accompanying tanks, would move at the maximum pace permitted by the vehicles. By making a concentrated attack these forces would be able to break through the enemy's defences into his territory and would then be able swiftly to dominate his defenceless homeland by taking command of the nerve centres. From this there developed the idea of the panzer division, the blitzkrieg and all the other versions of mobile warfare. The offence came into the ascendant.

The response in the Second World War was to use mobile forces for defence as well as offence in operations in which you sought, by use of a combination of prepared positions and manoeuvre, to trap the other side's forces, destroy them in a battle, and then advance. Offensive mobile forces were considered an essential means of defence, a position that was supported by the saying, for example, that 'the tank is the best weapon to destroy a tank'. The outcome of war tended to be determined by climactic battles, in which armoured forces and infantry fought together on each side, followed by long advances by the winning side. Against small countries a battle of this kind could be politically decisive: the whole country was overrun. Where spaces were large, the battles were decisive in a lesser degree: they determined which way the tide of war flowed.

The third technological era is hard to delineate since we are still going through it. It has witnessed a massive competition between the major powers in the application of science to destruction, a competition which was unleashed, or at least greatly intensified, by the development of nuclear weapons, and has spread to all types of weaponry. It can best be characterised as the era of electronics and atoms. At the sub-nuclear level, the important developments are a quite remarkable increase in the power

(1) to observe what is happening at short and long range by means of all kinds of sensors,
(2) to handle information in computers and communicate, and
(3) to guide munitions of short and long range with high accuracy at their targets.

Rocket propulsion has been improved and is used in missiles of all ranges. The increase in the lethality of sub-nuclear projectiles seems not to have been as striking as the increase in accuracy, apart from the development of munitions that cause indiscriminate damage to persons over an area, for example fuel-air explosives, anti-personnel cluster munitions, and the nerve gases. However, for the purpose of destroying hard targets, such as tanks, other motor vehicles, aircraft and ships or bridges, the great improvements in accuracy that are now occurring, plus the improvements – albeit more moderate – that are taking place in destructive power, are having the effect of greatly increasing the efficiency of sub-nuclear weapons.

Precision-guided munitions are coming along which possess a progressively higher kill probability, i.e. the probability that one shot will knock out the target at which it is aimed. These weapons can be designed for short- or long-range fire. Thus there are anti-tank

weapons of short range that are small and cheap, relative to the
armoured vehicles they are designed to attack, whilst long-range
'smart' missiles are being developed which are designed to release
many sub-munitions which will be programmed to guide themselves
at tanks or other targets, for example, aircraft. No doubt the future
will bring other devices that raise kill probabilities further.[9]

THE IMPLICATIONS OF INCREASED ACCURACY

With weapons of low kill probability it does not matter much who
shoots first. This is equally true of a confrontation between two men
with pistols in the Wild West, two bodies of infantry, two batteries of
artillery or any other two bodies of fighting men or fighting machines.
When accuracy is low, what matters is numerical superiority, i.e.
whether your side is firing more weapons at the enemy than he is
firing at you. For example, if, in an open shoot-out, you have twice as
many men as your opponent, two of your men can aim at each of his.
On the other hand, his men can aim at only half of your men. So at
the first round he will suffer a higher proportionate loss of men than
you, with the result that at the next round of fire the starting ratio of
men will be even more favourable to you, and so on. That is the basis
of the traditional law that it pays to concentrate your forces in order
to enjoy superior firepower, a law that was expressed in mathematics
by Lanchester early in this century.[10]

With high accuracy this proposition is reversed: as accuracy rises, it
matters more and more who shoots first; in the limiting case where
the kill probability is one, meaning that every shot is bound to hit and
destroy the target at which it is aimed, the outcome of a confrontation
between two men or two machines – aircraft, tanks or warships – will
depend only on who shoots first, nothing else. If A shoots first, B is
killed; if B shoots first, A is killed; if their shots cross in mid-air, both
A and B are killed. In this limiting case, there is no point in numerical
superiority in an engagement – as distinct from numerical superiority
in the total size of the forces of two nations or alliances. For if two
weapons with a kill probability of one are fired at a target, one is
wasted. There is no point in killing a target twice.

It follows that with weapons of high accuracy, it pays to be
concealed and invulnerable, so as to avoid being shot at first and be in
a position to shoot first – in other words, so as to gain the 'first shot

premium'. It pays to be dispersed for the sake of concealment and reduced vulnerability, rather than concentrated.[11]

Whether the trend to increased kill probabilities redounds to the benefit of attacker or defender depends first and foremost on who manages to gain the first shot premium. With surface warships, which cannot be concealed, the attacker is likely to reap the benefit, and the same goes for aircraft on airfields – though in both cases efforts can be made to reduce vulnerability by introducing defences and protection. Where, because of lack of concealment and protection, high accuracy benefits the attacker, it produces instability by increasing the pressure to attack pre-emptively.

With land forces, the defender enjoys the possibility, where suitable cover can be found or created, of using dispersed, concealed forces to lie in wait for the attacker, who must show himself in order to advance. This potential advantage for the defender is at the core of many of the models of defensive defence in land warfare. Where concealment and protection permit the defender to reap the first shot premium, the effect is stabilising: there is no pressure to attack pre-emptively.

AREA WEAPONS

A second trend has been the development of non-nuclear weapons that can knock out the forces of your opponent over a wide area, for example, chemical weapons, napalm, fuel-air weapons and clusters of anti-personnel bomblets. These result partly from the development of new killing agents and partly from developments in the range, accuracy and coverage of delivery systems – artillery, ground-launched missiles and air-launched missiles and bombs. The only possible ways to minimise the effects of attacks by these weapons are dispersion, to reduce the probability that your opponent will hit your forces, and protection, to reduce the chances that he will knock them out if he does hit them. The advent of tactical nuclear weapons was quickly recognised by military experts to mean that large concentrations of forces were no longer advisable; and the same principle has been swiftly recognised by all those subjected to non-nuclear area bombardment, for example the Vietnamese.

The ideal for the defender is to be able, from dispersed positions where his forces are relatively invulnerable, to bring concentrated fire to bear on an attacker wherever he manages to make headway by concentrating his forces – another principle used in models of defensive defence.

CLASSICAL LAWS

Ante-dating these propositions about current trends in technology, there is a set of classical propositions about the relative advantages of the defence and offence that are still germane.

First there is the proposition, which goes back to Clausewitz, that the defence is the stronger form of warfare for a set of unchanging reasons: the defender knows the terrain and can be dug in, whereas the attacker is in unfamiliar terrain and must show himself; the defender is supported by his own people; he can have prepositioned supplies to hand; and as he retreats his supply lines shorten, whilst those of the attacker increase, both with exponential effect, since as distance increases so does the amount of supplies required to support the men and animals or machines carrying supplies.

A modern manifestation of the classical advantages of the defender is the oft-stated rule of thumb that, to have a reasonable chance of success in a battle between all-round mobile forces, the attacker needs numerical superiority of 3 to 1 or more. This rule, derived from the experience of the Second World War, does not seem to have been radically modified since then.[12]

The attacker for his part has one great potential but uncertain advantage: the possibility of achieving surprise. To attack is to take the initiative; and to he who takes the initiative goes the possibility of surprise – though no certainty of achieving it.

THE REQUIREMENTS OF A DEFENSIVE STRUCTURE

With these general propositions in mind we can now specify the specific requirements of a defensive structure for non-nuclear forces and see how to satisfy them.

Requirement: crisis stability type 1 – avoid a race to mobilise. *Answer*: have forces *in situ*, partly professional, full-time forces (which in an alliance can include foreign troops), partly militia raised from the region. *Examples* Switzerland and Sweden. (The cost of militia forces is low.)

Requirement: crisis stability type 2 – avoid generating pressure to attack pre-emptively or the temptation to do so. *Answer*: reduce your offensive capability so that the other side does not fear pre-emptive attack; and design your forces so that they do not offer 'rich' targets that he might be tempted to attack, for example, vulnerable concentrations of forces, vulnerable supply lines, vulnerable command and control centres or other assets the elimination of which would cripple your capacity to defend yourself.

Requirement: escalation stability – avoid the risk that the use of nuclear weapons is forced on political leaders or occurs when it has not been sanctioned by them. *Answer*: acquire and train forces that have the capability to generate, without use of nuclear weapons, a stalemate and the prospect of a war of attrition; forces that can slow down, halt and press back the enemy in a manner that gives time for political processes; forces whose plans and training are not predicated on the use of nuclear weapons, but permit nuclear weapons to be truly in reserve as weapons of last resort, subject to absolute political control.

Requirement: minimise your capability to attack – *Answer*: minimise your reliance on mobile armoured forces; do not deploy logistics, bridging and other engineering equipment, or armoured forces you require for your defensive stance, in forward positions suitable for offensive operation; limit the reach of your forces into the territory of the other side; do not train and exercise your forces in the conduct of strategic offensive operations.

Requirement: maximise your capability to defend – *Answer*: prepare earthworks, barriers in depth, forested areas, fortifications and dispersed logistical supplies, and prepare passive munitions, for example, minefields and demolition charges or, exploiting modern technology, acquire weapons systems to dispense mines in the path of attacking forces. Use light infantry armed with anti-armour weapons, as well as anti-personnel weapons. Use simple remote control for anti-tank and similar weapons so that the soldiers who operate them are not too fearful of giving away their positions when they fire. Use command and communication systems with alternative links so that loss of command centres matters as little as possible. Avoid rigid linear defence with empty space behind it which produces the risk of breakthrough – but note that the Maginot Line was not broken through: it was outflanked. For bombardment of concentrations of attacking enemy forces, use dispersed launchers of modern smart munitions of limited range (so as not to reach far into the territory of the other side), and provide multiple communication systems so that there is a high chance that communications will not be severed. Invest in stocks and facilities required to permit the civilian population to survive – stocks of foods, medicines, fuel and other essential supplies, shelters, reserve generators – and ensure that the peacetime infrastructure of the economy is designed with a view to assisting survival in war, for example telecommunications, transport, food storage and hospitals.

It is not too difficult to develop principles of this kind on the basis of which the offensive capability of *land* forces can be reduced and their defensive capability increased, or *vice versa*, within limits dictated by geography: the greater the area to be defended and the better the natural cover and natural obstacles, the greater will be the scope for a defensive posture, which inevitably means some temporary loss of territory.

To put the point rather differently, one can see that in the design of land forces, in the acquisition of new weapons and new infrastructure, including earthworks and fortifications, and in the development of doctrine on how to fight, there is some freedom to choose between a more offensive or a more defensive stance. Whether they know it or not, those who make decisions about military programmes in our countries are making this choice all the time. Very probably they scarcely know it, since in most countries it has been virtually taken for granted that the greater the offensive strength of the armed forces the more effective they will be, without reference to political aims.

In applying these principles it is necessary to distinguish between levels of military activity and consider the alternative policies and force structures available at each level and how policy at one level dictates that at another.

It is customary to distinguish three levels – the strategic, operational and tactical.

The strategic level concerns what is to be the military objective in the event of war; the operational level concerns how each large body of forces is to operate in pursuit of that strategic objective or basket of alternative strategic objectives; and the tactical level concerns how each small unit is to fight so as to achieve what is required at the operational level.

The choice at the strategic level (based firmly on a political choice) sets the guidelines for the choice at the operational level, which in turn sets the guidelines for the choice at the tactical level. Conversely, what is decided at the tactical level will set bounds to the possible choices at the operational level, and what is decided at the operational level will set bounds to the strategic choices. Causation flows both ways.

The choice of how you plan to execute that strategy at the operational and tactical levels constitutes your military doctrine, if the choices are sufficiently coherent to justify the use of the word doctrine. (Where that is not so, military traditions rule.)

Our concern is with the ways in which this hierarchy of choices can be shifted between an offensive and a defensive orientation.

At the strategic level two Soviet analysts have pointed to the distinction between four possible non-nuclear strategies.[13]

You may plan to:

1. attack pre-emptively or in cold blood;
2. respond to an attack against you by defensive–offensive operations in which you aim to check the attack and swiftly go over to a retaliatory attack so as to punish your opponent or achieve other gains;
3. respond by defensive operations and counter-attacks which go only as far as the frontier; or
4. respond to attack by defensive operations, making limited counter-attacks if any, with the aim of producing a stalemate in which to seek a political solution to whatever the fighting is about.

At the operational level, which determines how each large body of forces operates, you will plan for offensive as well as defensive operations if you pursue any of the strategies 1–3, but the emphasis on the offensive will diminish as you go from 1 to 3. For strategy 4, planning will be mainly for defensive operations.

At the tactical level, if we define it sufficiently narrowly in terms of the size of the unit considered, you will always want to have an ability to go over to the offensive locally whatever the objective that is being pursued at the operational or strategic levels. For example, if one part of a line you are holding is yielding, you will wish to be able to push back the attacker by local counter-attack: you will wish to be able to take the initiative locally.

If the wholly defensive strategy were adopted – strategy 4 on the list above – the attributes of the units at the tactical level would be such that the possibilities of pursuing strategies 3, 2 or 1 would be small – and progressively smaller in that order. For at the tactical level there would not be strong mobile armoured units, nor would the forces be trained, deployed and equipped for major offensive operations or major counter-offensive operations.

With strategy 3 – which requires a limited counter-attack capability to the frontier – the offensive component would be increased and the question has to be addressed whether there is a significant and visible distinction between the characteristics of forces designed for this strategy and those designed for strategies 2 and 1.

This is a matter that requires expert appraisal. The starting point from which it appears appropriate that such an appraisal should start is that strategic offensive operations, and to a lesser extent defensive–offensive operations at the strategic level, require an ability to manage large bodies of troops in rapidly changing, fluid warfare; which in turn requires combat troops who are highly trained in this type of warfare and are in a high state of readiness; which requires that large troop exercises and headquarters exercises be conducted with considerable frequency. Further it is necessary to have the infrastructure for offensive operations, such as forward deployment of special equipment and ammunition.

From the extent to which forces possess characteristics of this kind it should be possible for experts to say that they have a greater or lesser capability for offensive operations. What matters is the totality of everything that can be subsumed under the word doctrine: the declared aims, methods of fighting, equipment, training, logistics and economic backing of a nation's forces.

There is inertia in doctrine. It will take time for new ideas to be adopted at the top and, once adopted, it will take still more time for them to be assimilated into staff colleges, training manuals, deployments, equipment and training. It follows that in order to appraise the doctrine of a nation, rather than look just at the characteristics of its forces at a moment in time, which will reflect the decisions of former years, it is important to look for signs of change at all levels, from policy statements at the top, to the new equipment being developed and acquired, to the visible characteristics of the forces, including any changes in their deployment, training and infrastructure. To watch doctrine change in peacetime will be like watching a large ship change course. There will be a lag between a turn on the wheel and the response of the vessel. In wartime, defeat can prompt more rapid response.

So far we have considered land forces.

AIR FORCES

Air forces perform two functions that influence the outcome of a war – reconnaissance and bombardment. Bombardment can be of two types: the bombing of your opponent's army and navy and their installations so as to reduce their capacity to fight, and, secondly, 'strategic' bombing of your opponent's economy and people, in the hope of breaking his economic capacity to fight and the psychological will of his people to do so.[14]

But a major part of the effort of an air force goes not into these functions that may directly affect the outcome of a war, but into the task of destroying the opponent's air force by attacking it on the ground or in the air. That is necessary in order to prevent your opponent's air force performing its functions of reconnaissance and bombardment against your surface forces – and to prevent it obstructing your air force in the performance of those tasks against his surface forces. Since the purpose of each air force is to knock out the other side's air force and achieve air superiority, there is strong pressure to attack his air force pre-emptively: air forces produce crisis instability. Moreoever nothing in the arms race is more extravagant than the creation of large air forces waiting to attack each other and likely in the early stages of a war to suffer huge combined losses as they fight for air superiority.

It can well be argued that reconnaissance and bombardment, which are what air forces contribute to the outcome of a war – in contrast to which destroying each other's aeroplanes is merely an expensive preliminary step – can be done increasingly economically by unmanned vehicles and missiles and that manned aircraft are therefore becoming obsolete. Moreover unmanned vehicles which can be launched from dispersed mobile launchers are less vulnerable than manned aircraft that require airfields and runways. They therefore give rise to less risk of pre-emptive attack – though vertical take-off aircraft are less vulnerable than traditional types of aircraft.

On the other hand, whatever their cost-effectiveness, it will take time to overcome institutional resistance to the reduction and abolition of air forces, just as it took time to get rid of the cavalry. Meanwhile one must consider how air forces fit into the alternative strategies with which we are concerned.

There are two stylised facts which we take as starting points:

1. If we leave aside long-range bombers, which have largely been

displaced by ballistic missiles, aircraft are in a considerable degree multi-purpose, i.e. they can be used for attack against ground targets or for defence, meaning to attack enemy aircraft in the air. Yet some aircraft are designed and equipped for attack and some for defence; and their equipment and logistics, and also the training of their crews, will be directed to the fulfilment of offensive or defensive tasks in a manner that is not immediately flexible. Hence it is possible to vary attack and defence capabilities, albeit in a manner that may not be simple to define.

2. Compared with the early days of aviation the technical difference between military and civil aircraft has increased to the point where the possibilities of adapting civil aircraft to military uses other than transport has become slight, perhaps negligible.

This means that one side on its own has the ability within significant limits to alter the structure of its air force between attack and defence capabilities, as specified by reference to the technical capability of its aircraft, the training of their crews and their logistics. But that is not the end of the story. To concentrate on defensive capabilities is to deny yourself two capabilities that may be important to the conduct of a defensive war. The first is the capability of attack aircraft swiftly to bombard enemy land forces at any point where they are making progress. We can call this lateral mobility of attack. Aircraft are well suited to this task because they can be concentrated swiftly and are most effective against concentrated targets.[15] The second is the ability to attack the enemy's air force on the ground by striking his air bases.

The time will come, and may indeed be upon us, when both these and the other functions of aircraft can best be performed by unmanned vehicles. The classic argument that a pilot has the ability to pick 'targets of opportunity' and can be diverted to new targets while airborne must be losing strength as technology brings improvements in surveillance and in missiles. Whichever side first adopts the policy of relying on unmanned vehicles only will reap the advantage, until his opponent adopts the same policy, of being able to shoot at any aircraft that passes over – or at least any aircraft coming from the enemy area – on the safe assumption that it is an enemy aircraft, whereas when manned aircraft are possessed by both sides the difficulty of discriminating between friendly and hostile aircraft, both making round trips, is such that it will often happen that hostile aircraft pass freely and friendly aircraft are shot down. The abandonment of manned combat aircraft might be a more complete solution to the hitherto intractable problem of identifying friend and foe (the IFF problem) in wartime conditions than any that technology, always vulnerable to counter-measures, seems likely to offer.

But these are all developments in the future. In present circumstances, the scope for unilateral action to reduce the offensive capability of air forces is limited though not negligible. The greater the capability for attack and the range of your air force the more will your opponent feel the need to acquire defence capabilities in the form of interceptor aircraft and ground-to-air defences, and the more he may feel obliged to acquire attack capabilities with which to strike your aircraft on the ground: the greater will be instability. Restraint in the acquisition of attack aircraft, and reciprocal reductions in their numbers, will help stability.

As unmanned missiles – ballistic missiles and cruise missiles – replace aircraft as instruments of bombardment, the same principles should be applied to them: avoid those that enhance your capacity to attack, especially those that are vulnerable; and go for those that enhance your capacity to defend but be sure not to undermine your opponent's capacity to defend. These principles may not be easy to put into practice one-sidedly. The best solution appears to be to limit the range of missiles so that they can be used against forces when they attack, or when they concentrate prior to attack, but cannot reach deep into your opponent's defensive system, assuming it has substantial depth.

The renunciation of the capacity for long-range bombardment would mean that you could not bombard your opponent's lines of reinforcement at 'choke points', nor his headquarters and command and control systems. Since bombardment of targets of these kinds can be perceived as a contribution to both your defensive capability and your offensive capability, it is hard to say how far it would be possible to go one-sidedly in renouncing this capability. Clearly it is desirable to exercise restraint, since dual-purpose capabilities of this kind can generate fear of attack and be destabilising.

NAVIES

Apart from submarines carrying long-range nuclear missiles, warships in general serve to attack other warships, to attack merchant shipping or to attack targets on shore. Almost any warship, whether it carries guns, mines, missiles or aircraft as means of bombardment, can perform all these functions, though it will be designed primarily for one function rather than another. Since the only way one warship can impede another is by attacking it, there can be no distinction between offensive and defensive naval capabilities (other than mines), though the range of warships and their supporting facilities dictates how far from home they operate.[16]

Surface ships are increasingly vulnerable to precision-guided munitions fired from ships, submarines, aircraft and shore; and, as with air forces, there is strong pressure to attack pre-emptively so as to gain command of the seas – the equivalent of gaining air superiority – before the other side attacks you. There is inherent crisis instability.

The only effective step that can be taken unilaterally to improve stability is to reduce dependence on the seas by stockpiling imported food, fuels, raw materials and manufactured products essential to the conduct of war – and to avoid dependence on troop reinforcements from abroad – or to rely on forms of transport other than shipping if they are less vulnerable. The shorter war is likely to be, the more valuable will stock-piling be as a means of diminishing your vulnerability and discouraging your neighbour from attacking you.

For evidence on the feasibility of defensive force structures and their cost we can look to several sources – the experience of countries that possess defensive forces, the results of modelling and of military exercises.

EVIDENCE FROM NON-ALIGNED COUNTRIES

In Europe the non-aligned countries generally have defensive strategies of necessity: they are too small to attack or threaten to attack the larger powers which might be tempted to invade them, most probably in the course of a general European war. Their object is to dissuade a potential invader by raising the costs he would incur if he attacked. They generally rely heavily on defence in depth, but they typically posssess significant mobile armoured forces for use in areas where mobile defence appears best.[17] In other words, their doctrine is pragmatic and is not generally shaped by insistence on being defensive on moral or political grounds at the operational level. For example, Sweden does not appear in its military planning to pay much attention to the question whether the forces it acquires have an offensive capability *vis-à-vis* its immediate neighbours, Finland and Norway. Greater Swedish military strength, whatever its nature, appears to be regarded by its neighbours as an asset that will diminish the risk of Soviet intrusion into Scandinavia in the event of crisis or war, not as a threat to them. In what amounts to an implicit alliance of nations with common interests, faith in the peaceful political intentions of Sweden is such that its military capabilities are not critically and fearfully examined by its neighbours for evidence of offensive potential. All the same Swedish forces are not designed for a strategic offensive; and the Swiss explicitly take the view that the Swiss model is 'badly suited to take the offensive into the depths of the enemy's rear area'.[18]

The military expenditures of the non-aligned countries are not high, yet their military forces are large. In the six non-aligned countries, Austria, Finland, Ireland, Sweden, Switzerland and Yugoslavia, military expenditure exceeds 3 per cent of the gross domestic product (GDP) in only one, Yugoslavia, where the GDP is low and, consequently, the burden of maintaining modern arms is great. The average ratio of military expenditure to GDP is significantly lower in the non-aligned countries than in the member countries of the two alliances.

As a measure of the potential strength of these countries, Sweden, with a population of 8 million, has a mobilisation strength of 800,000 in 72 hours. Switzerland, with a population of 6 million, has a mobilisation strength of 1.1 million, including 460,000 civil defence workers, in 48 hours. Sweden has an air force of 501 combat aircraft. For comparison, Britain with a population of 56 million has 300,000 active members in its armed forces with another 300,000 in reserve, and the Royal Air Force has 596 aircraft.[19] Both Sweden and Switzerland have had a policy of investing in facilities designed to permit the nation to hold out for a long time in the event of war, such as modern shelters for the mass of the population, emergency medical and communication facilities, and stocks of imports and war supplies. In Switzerland the total length of underground ammunition chambers alone is some 80 kilometres (50 miles).[20] The policy of both countries – and of all the neutrals – is to dissuade a potential attacker by making invasion look as if it would lead to a long war of attrition and hence be too costly in relation to its possible benefits.

The main reasons for the high apparent cost-effectiveness of the forces of these neutral countries are these:

1. Great reliance is placed on militia troops who, after a period of training as conscripts, are recalled for regular short periods of training and are always ready, with their arms close at hand, to take their places at short notice in the defence of the nation. Since as conscripts or reservists they receive little pay, the cost of manpower in the military budget is low. The effectiveness of these troops for offensive operations requiring intense training will surely be less than that of professional full-time armies, but with their knowledge of the country and their large numbers, they may be effective in the tasks for which they are designed.

2. Much of the expenditure to enhance the capacity to hold out in a war has been spread over a long time and is in the nature of an investment with a long life before it needs replacement or updating. Consider, for example, expenditure to ensure that every new building has provision for shelter and survival, that road bridges are prepared for demolition charges as they are built, that communication systems are hardened and made adaptable to military use, that emergency generators are ready, and that underground stores are built to hold sufficient supplies of food, fuel and other materials for the population to be able to survive for a considerable period. These are the kind of long-life facilities in which these two countries have invested gradually over a long period.

What the evidence from the non-aligned countries suggests is that a strong defensive stance need not have a high budgetary cost in the long run, but that it requires political support for extended compulsory service in militia forces and it requires willing participation by civilians in supporting services. Moreover an attempt to reproduce the defensive forces and infrastructure of Sweden or Switzerland in a short period could be very expensive for a country which, starting from a different tradition, had not invested in the infrastructure and training that is required and lacked the political tradition of willing participation in the defence of the nation for the sake of its neutrality and autonomy. If, as is now the case for NATO and the WTO, there is a choice between achieving defensive superiority by building up defensive forces or by reciprocal reductions in offensive forces, the latter is clearly to be strongly to be preferred on economic grounds, quite apart from any other grounds.

EVIDENCE FROM MODELLING

Computer modelling of military operations is probably not a very reliable guide to reality, since the answers it produces are determined by the assumptions that are fed into the models as they are constructed and by the way in which the models are subsequently adjusted so as to make the model produce results that are plausible to the operator. But modelling by experts in West Germany is reported to have shown that dispersed defensive networks are rather effective against mobile armoured attack.[21]

THE EFFICACY OF DENIAL AND RETALIATION

It is impossible to say whether in a nuclear setting a non-nuclear strategy of denial or a non-nuclear strategy of retaliation will be more effective (at a given cost) in dissuading an opponent from attack if he has aggressive intentions. With the first it is the prospect of a war of attrition in a nuclear setting that is relied upon to dissuade. With the second it is the prospect that there will be a mobile war in which there is a substantial probability that one side or other will win a decisive victory which will lead to the use of nuclear weapons by the loser.

Since nuclear weapons were introduced, reliance on the threat of retaliation as a means of dissuasion, which is the only possible means of dissuasion with nuclear weapons, has spilled over into discussion of non-nuclear strategy, obscuring the possible effectiveness of the threat of attrition.

The First World War was a classic, appalling example of a war of attrition. The advent of mobile armoured warfare and the blitzkrieg in the Second World War revived the notion of quick, clean campaigns in which political aims might be achieved at low, or at least acceptable, cost. Mearsheimer has well argued that in modern times war has been attractive when there has been a good chance that a blitzkrieg will succeed and unattractive when the likely outcome has been a war of attrition. In his words, 'the threat of war of attrition is the bedrock of conventional deterrence'.[22]

Recently there have been conspicuous examples of how armies which possess modern equipment for mobile war can become bogged down in wars of attrition. Vietnam and Afghanistan are examples where guerilla-type resistance has been effective, indeed victorious at terrible cost. The Iran–Iraq war is an example where orthodox military forces, each with much modern equipment obtained from abroad, became bogged down in a war of attrition with huge costs in bloodshed and military expenditure. On the other hand, Israel provides an example of successful though costly blitzkriegs and, perhaps, an example of how the threat of retaliation with non-nuclear forces (backed by increasingly credible rumours of nuclear weapons) can dissuade.

While it is impossible to see a basis for saying whether non-nuclear denial or retaliation, where geography offers some choice between them, is generally a more effective means of dissuasion, viewed from the perspective of which of the two will more effectively keep a hostile neighbour at bay *in the short run*, it can be said that, viewed in a wider and longer perspective, retaliation is less stable than denial and it has unfavourable rather than favourable feedback into political relations and competition in arms.

One argument that has been made against denial is that, if a nation A adopts a defensive strategy, its neighbour B can confidently take a slice of A's territory near the frontier because A has limited offensive forces with which to re-take that slice – or take a slice of B's territory to trade against the slice which A has lost. Another way of putting the argument is that, if A had stronger offensive forces and could counter-attack or attack more effectively at the non-nuclear level, B would be running higher risks if it attempted to take a slice of territory. Insofar as B, the potential attacker, judged the case for a non-nuclear attack of this kind in a nuclear setting purely by the chances of local success with his non-nuclear forces in being, this argument would have force – though this would apply equally to a situation where A's limited capacity to attack was the result not of possessing forces that were defensive but of possessing all-round forces that were small relatively to B's forces. But whatever type of forces A possessed, B, the attacker, would have to consider whether resistance by B within the area taken, and harassment at its boundaries, would not preclude a clean, decisive outcome and mean that there was a risk of getting involved in a war of attrition with the risk of escalation never totally absent.

THE TRANSITION TO DEFENSIVENESS

A transition by one nation or alliance on its own from reliance on offensive mobile forces towards increased reliance on defensive forces of limited mobility is not simple in its effects on stability. If, starting with a force comprising mobile armoured forces, you introduce barriers, for example minefields, at one part of your frontier and do not reduce those armoured forces, one effect will be to free some of them from the task of supporting the defence of that area and make them available to join a concentration of forces for offensive operations at another part of the frontier, thus enhancing your offensive potential.[23] In this way the introduction of defences can be menacing, unless it is accompanied by changes in doctrine, deployments, force structures and weapons that clearly demonstrate a change in the overall capabilities of the forces towards the defensive. The removal of offensive elements (with no increase in defensive capabilities) is more stabilising, and more likely to be seen to be stabilising, than the addition of defensive elements in substitution for offensive elements; but it may require bilateral action, a subject we deal with in the next section.

The choice between emphasis on the defensive and offensive is not something to be addressed only at those infrequent intervals when the political aims and military strategy of a nation or alliance are reviewed – when, as rarely happens, it reconsiders its military doctrine. The choice should be addressed every time consideration is given to such matters as what new weapons to develop and buy, how best to train troops, how to deploy them, and what should be the relative size of different branches of the armed forces and different types of unit within those branches. Day to day decisions about these matters will determine how defensive or offensive is the force structure. In the absence of clear political guidance that penetrates all practice to be governed by two tendencies: the tendency to perpetuate tradition; and the tendency to think that the more firepower a weapon has the better, without regard to the effect the weapon has on the offensive and defensive capabilities of the forces.

THE ONE-SIDED CASE: CONCLUSION

The following conclusions seem possible:

1. Nations can choose, within limits dictated by geography and technology, between land forces designed with offensive emphasis and land forces designed with defensive emphasis: they can thus choose between emphasis on retaliation and emphasis on denial by war of attrition. As regards geography, Israel, for example, is so small that it probably has rather little scope for a defensive stance compared with larger countries; Europe is better placed but still does not have great space.

2. There is much less scope for changing the structure of air forces and navies. But land forces are the heart of the matter. Air forces and navies, using non-nuclear weapons, can do great damage by bombardment and blockade, but they are unlikely to have a quick, decisive effect on the outcome of a war in the absence of land forces that can advance and take territory.

3. Comparison of the military expenditures of non-allied countries in Europe and those of countries in the alliances indicates that, over a long period, the costs of the two strategies are not decisively different: defensive strategies are significantly cheaper in terms of budgetary costs in relation to GDP, but they entail larger unpaid contributions and indirect costs (which are not readily measurable); and they require investment in defensive infrastructure, which is a moderate burden if spread over a long period but would be a heavy burden if undertaken quickly.

4. It is impossible to say whether denial or retaliation will be a more effective short-run strategy (at a given cost) for dissuading a potential enemy from attack; but a defensive strategy will be better than an offensive strategy for stability and feedback: it will provide greater crisis stability and escalation stability; it will provide a greater opportunity for a confrontation to be ended and competition in arms reversed, if your opponent, like you, has peaceful intentions.

5. A transition by one country from offensiveness to defensiveness can appear menacing to a neighbour and hence be destabilising if it is not achieved by reductions in offensive forces that substantially outweigh the additions, if any, that are made to defensive forces.

THE TWO-SIDED CASE

As soon as we address the idea that, in order to settle their differences, both parties to a confrontation might in unison adopt the objective of Mutual Defensive Superiority, the problem is transformed: many of the difficulties resolve themselves, and most criticisms levelled at the one-sided introduction of defensive defence become irrelevant.[24] Instead of trying to introduce defences that will stand up to offensive forces, the task is to remove offensive capabilities on both sides while initially keeping defensive forces intact; the further offensive capabilities are reduced the greater will be the dominance of the defence and the greater will be the scope for reductions in defensive components consistent with the maintenance of security; in place of costs of change, there is the possibility of immediate savings; and logically the need for any armed forces, other than those required for internal law and order, collapses.

The two-sided approach has sometimes been called transarmament. It is a variant of qualitative disarmament which was tried in the early 1930s. When Germany after defeat was disarmed in 1918, all her armed forces were reduced to a minimum and she was totally forbidden weapons such as tanks and military aircraft which might give her the capability to attack others. The idea that, in generalising disarmament to other nations, offensive weapons should be removed was proposed during the preparations for the 1932 Disarmament Conference and then taken up at that conference.

The failure of the qualitative approach in 1932–33 has generally been attributed to political causes, but it is sometimes said that the conference would have failed anyway because its experts found it impossible to distinguish offensive from defensive weapons; and it is further suggested that this difficulty is a permanent, insurmountable obstacle to the qualitative approach.

When the record is examined, as it is in an Appendix to this essay, this last conclusion does not stand up. It is true that the Technical Commissions appointed by the Conference failed to agree on distinctions between offensive and defensive weapons, but they addressed the wrong question – a misorientation of their work which might not have occurred if there had been more political will to obtain results. The experts were asked what weapons were offensive, a question which offers great scope for disagreement and obfuscation when it is cast, as it was, in general terms and leaves open the question whether one or both parties to any potential conflict is going to give up the weapons classified as offensive. For, just as the laying of a minefield can augment the offensive potential of a nation's forces by releasing mobile forces to take part in an offensive, so almost any weapon will enhance, directly or indirectly, the offensive (and defensive) potential of a nation's forces in some circumstances.

The correct question to ask is, are there components of the strategy, stance and structure, including weapons, of the armed forces which if removed from *both* parties to a confrontation will reduce the offensive capability of each relative to the defensive capability of the other? The point of reformulating the question in this way is twofold: to focus on two-sided change; and to emphasise the need to consider all the components that make up the offensive relative to defensive capabilities of the two sides under consideration, not just the weapons.

At this point it is useful to consider some general propositions concerning the logic of the two-sided approach.

- It is always possible to achieve Mutual Defensive Superiority by reciprocal (but not necessarily identical) restructuring, provided that on each side some units are, or can be, restructured so as to be better at defence than offence. (If there were only units that were at least as good at offence as defence, it would of course be impossible to achieve Mutual Defensive Superiority.)

- If the defensive units consist of dispersed and concealed forces which seek to gain the first-shot premium, an all-round reduction in numbers of defensive and offensive forces on both sides will tend to bring a disproportionate advantage at the tactical level to the defender, in terms of the rate at which he will inflict casualties relative to the rate at which the attacker will do so. The tactical level here means the range within which each side can see and hit the other side in the absence of concealment. The reason for the gain to the defender is that as numbers go down the attacker's rate of kill goes down because his rate of detection of the defender is reduced *both* by the reduction in the number of his forces attempting to detect defenders and by the number of defenders to be detected. On the other hand, if the defenders, *ex hypothesi*, can see all the attackers within range, their rate of kill is reduced only by the reduction in their own numbers.[25]

This proposition needs to be used with caution. In particular, it depends on the range being equal at which the two sides, in the absence of concealment, can detect and hit each other with the weapons at their disposal. Nevertheless it is an important corrective to the notion that there is a minimum 'force-to-space ratio' of defending forces needed to stop an attack, below which it is not safe to reduce the density of your own forces. To suggest that the size of the forces you need to stop an attack does not depend on the size and character of your opponent's forces is absurd, and it is a travesty of the thinking of the father of the force-to-space ratio, Liddell Hart. He, encouraged by T. E. Lawrence, used the notion of the force-to-space ratio to help explain the experience of armies in battle since the Napoleonic wars, but he ended his analysis arguing strongly that rules of thumb 'in which the norm is apt to be a product of custom and habit' should be replaced by the use of scientifically analysed data.[26]

– If the size of the forces of one side significantly exceeds the size of the other, the achievement of Mutual Defensive Superiority requires that the stronger side should reduce its offensive strength to *below* the initial defensive strength of the weaker side, and that the weaker side reduce its offensive strength if that is needed to ensure that they are not superior to the defensive forces of the stronger. If the stronger side simply reduces its forces across the board to the point where they are equal in both defensive and offensive strength to the forces of the weaker side, the result will be a balance of forces and that, as we have seen, is a condition of instability.

Indeed to move from a position of imbalance to a balance of forces, by force increases by the weaker side or by force reductions by the stronger side, will make the position less, not more, stable. For if one country is indisputably stronger in non-nuclear forces than its neighbour, for example, the Soviet Union *vis-à-vis* Finland, the United States *vis-à-vis* Canada or Britain *vis-à-vis* Ireland, there can be a stable peace if the stronger is content with the status quo. But if Finland, Canada and Ireland were as large as their neighbours and had equally strong non-nuclear forces, mutual suspicion as to the motives for which the (equal) forces were kept could sour relations between each pair of neighbours, leading to mutual fear of attack and hence crisis instability and competition in arms. Or, to cite an American military analyst, if NATO had mobile armoured forces equal to those of the WTO, 'it would not be unreasonable to assume that in a crisis, serious consideration would be given to striking first. Thus a highly unstable situation would obtain, since both the Pact and NATO would be considering offensive operations'.[27] As noted in Chapter 2, balance in all-round forces or offensive forces is unstable. For these reasons, the aim from the start of a bilateral policy for the two-sided pursuit of defensiveness should be to remove offensive capabilities to the point where Mutual Defensive Superiority is achieved. If the forces of one side are initially stronger than those of the other, what is needed are single asymmetric steps sufficiently large to produce Mutual Defensive Superiority. This does not mean that only the stronger side should cut its forces. Unless it has negligible offensive forces, the weaker side should reduce or remove its offensive capabilities too for two reasons. In the first place, it is important that in the first step the asymmetric actions should together produce Mutual Defensive Superiority by as large a margin as possible. Secondly, it will be easier for the stronger side to accept asymmetric cuts in its offensive capabilities if the weaker side does something than if it does nothing.

THE APPROACH TO RESTRUCTURING

How then should restructuring be approached? What are the concrete steps each side should take, singly or in concert with the other? Essentially there are five.

The first step is to change doctrine so that thinking at all levels is guided by the right objectives and concepts: the achievement of stability and positive feedback by removing what is offensive and threatening to the other side and keeping what is defensive and reassuring to him.

The second step, which can take place before or after changes in the physical composition of forces have begun, is to increase mutual confidence by measures such as being open with information about military matters, avoiding exercises that can be construed as evidence that you might attack or that you seek an offensive capability, permitting the observation of exercises and the verification of disarmament agreements, and redeploying assault forces away from the frontier. A successful example of arrangements of this kind is to be found in the arrangements for the withdrawal of forces, in particular those with an offensive capability, from the Israeli–Syrian border on the Golan Heights. This arrangement has been in operation under United Nations supervision since 1974.[28]

The third step is to get rid of the offensive components of the forces by selectively disbanding troops, destroying weapons and destroying infrastructure and any other assets required for the offensive.

The fourth step is to reduce force levels of all kinds and military spending as the mutual military threat is removed by the process of restructuring.

The fifth step is to refrain from developing and acquiring new types of weapon that are primarily offensive to replace those that have been abandoned.

From the discussion earlier in this chapter it is pretty clear that with land forces there can be a considerable degree of choice between forces with offensive and defensive capability; with air forces there is some choice but not much; and with navies there is little choice, if any. It follows that, for two nations or alliances to achieve Mutual Defensive Superiority by reciprocal actions, the appropriate pattern for their actions is that they remove the offensive components of their land forces, thereby achieving Mutual Defensive Superiority on land, and they should reduce, and eventually eliminate, their air forces and navies so that these two largely unrestructurable forces cease to generate mutual threats and instability in the air and sea, and cease to threaten to upset the defensive superiority established on land by the removal of offensive components from the land forces.

With these steps it should logically be possible to unwind a two-party military confrontation and reduce forces to zero. At least these are the reciprocal steps that would be appropriate to two nations seeking to unwind a military confrontation, achieve reassurance and disarm. They should be envisaged as part and parcel of a process of political reconciliation in which the armed forces were being made defensive and reduced, economic and social relations were being opened up and actions in all fields were moving together. If all the parts do not move together, the whole process is not likely to succeed. If the parts do move together they will reinforce each other: as trust increases through more working and social contacts, and common economic interests are increased, it will be easier to agree on force reductions and their enforcement, and conversely the steps taken to ease the military confrontation will help the improvement of economic and political relations. Cumulative causation is likely to operate. But this does not mean that, once started, the process of unwinding a confrontation will necessarily roll forward smoothly and will never roll backwards.

THE OUT OF AREA PROBLEM

We have so far discussed the adoption of defensive non-nuclear strategies by two countries. The difficulties of introducing defensive strategies when there are more than two countries (or geographically united alliances) were discussed in Chapter 2. The most severe problem, it will be recalled, occurs if there is a strong country in the middle – Germany earlier in this century is the classic example – whose forces have a significant offensive capability: its neighbours on either side (France and Russia before 1914) may feel obliged to acquire forces with an offensive capability so that if the central power attacks one of them, the other can help by joining in and attacking the central power from the other side.

As you increase the number of countries who may combine against any one, so the chances of achieving military stability diminish. But the more defensive the forces of each nation, measured by the ratio of its defensive to its offensive capability, the less likely is a combination of them against one to enjoy offensive superiority.

Another, similar, problem is that of 'out of area' forces. This has two aspects. First, a large nation with forces on several widely separated frontiers (e.g. the Soviet Union) or forces stationed abroad on the territory of allies far from the home country (e.g. the United States) may have forces outside the area to which agreed reciprocal measures to reduce offensive capabilities are to be applied (e.g. Europe). In that event, restraints on the introduction of forces from outside the area may need to be considered, or perhaps a ceiling on the out of area forces – though that line of argument quickly leads to the politically unenforceable view that, if one part of the world is to be disarmed, partially or wholly, the whole world must be disarmed in the same degree.

The second aspect of the problem is that nations which in the old days wished to police their empires, and nations that nowadays wish to 'project power', have felt the need to keep mobile offensive forces for this purpose. This indeed was one of the obstacles to qualitative disarmament raised by Britain in 1932. The question today is whether this is an obstacle to the pursuit of defensiveness within a region such as Europe. There is no technical obstacle to prevent a nation keeping forces with offensive orientation for use in one part of the world and forces with a defensive orientation for use in another. But there are likely to be political and institutional obstacles to the adoption of a two-doctrine approach of that kind. Nations and their armed forces tend to have a single dominant vision of their role in the world. The European neutrals have one vision. They are defensive and insofar as they train troops for service abroad, they train them for peace-keeping duties with the United Nations. France and Britain, two ex-imperial powers have another vision, which includes minor excursions abroad to deal with the residues of empire. The United States has another in which the need to project power and defend vital interests is powerfully proclaimed. In the Soviet Union, doctrine appears to be in flux, moving from power projection towards non-intervention. Beneath these broad visions, there are training manuals, training exercises and deployments which tend to contain a single vision of how to fight. To get acceptance of the notion that it may be appropriate to have two different doctrines for different parts of the world and to get those alternatives translated into training manuals, force structures and into the whole structure of military preparations is not likely to be an easy task. It may be easier for allies from outside an area where defensive strategies are being adopted, for example, the United States if NATO adopts defensive doctrine, to reduce their presence as the confrontation is unwound, leaving responsibility for defence of the area more and more in the hands of local nations who do not plan substantially for military operations outside the area and who can therefore adopt a defensive strategy without ambivalence.

5 The Implementation of a Strategy

Whether and at what price it will be possible for a country or alliance to achieve its desired military stance will depend upon its own actions and on the reactions of its opponent. The actions that can be taken by *one* side have been explored in previous chapters. This chapter considers what one side can do through its military policies to influence the actions of the other side in a manner favourable to the achievement of its objectives. International policies of a non-military kind – for example steps to open or close economic relations – are beyond the scope of this enquiry but, as has been emphasised before in this essay, their great importance in the attainment of international political objectives should never be forgotten, nor should it be supposed that military policy can be conducted in isolation from non-military policies. The two go together.

THREE METHODS OF IMPLEMENTATION

There are three principal methods by which a nation or alliance may influence the military strategy and arms policy of another:[1]

1. By *independent acts* of arms policy, i.e. by unilaterally changing its strategy and the level and characteristics of its forces, nuclear and non-nuclear, so that they demonstrate what are its possible actions.
2. By *discussion*, i.e. by discussing with the other side, and by discussing in domestic forums which the other side can follow, the logic and merits of alternative strategies and force structures and the possible steps each can take, and proposes to take, towards those objectives.
3. By *negotiation*, i.e. by attempting to strike bargains in which a change in arms policy is made conditional on a change by the other side, on the grounds that it is not in your interest to modify your policy unless the other side reciprocates by doing likewise.

74

The process here called discussion could be described as positive dialogue: one side says, I am going independently to undertake these steps which will make us both more secure; I suggest you take similar steps for the same purpose. The exchange is primarily informative and persuasive in design. Conversely, the term negative dialogue could be applied to negotiation, a process in which one side says to the other, I will not do this unless you do that, thus putting both parties into adversarial postures, like squabbling children.

How should a choice be made between the three approaches?

We are concerned with a nation (or alliance) in a nuclear setting which has come to recognise that its political aims must be peaceful; its strategy is therefore to seek, in combination, a nuclear stance of Sufficiency and a non-nuclear stance of Defensive Superiority; it seeks to reassure, not to deceive; it seeks to induce the other side to move in the same direction so that progressively the two sides may together undo the confrontation and end competition in arms. This basic principle suggests itself:

> If there is a change in the structure of the nation's (or alliance's) forces that would help it attain its desired military stance, *regardless of whether the other side makes a similar move*, it has no grounds for seeking reciprocity through negotiation.

If we ignore costs, we can say that if one side, country A, whose aims are peaceful, has nuclear forces which in quantity or quality are inconsistent with Sufficiency or it has non-nuclear forces the structure of which is offensive, it will be able to improve stability and feedback without reciprocity from country B, if it can and does change the level and structure of those forces in the direction of nuclear Sufficiency and non-nuclear Defensive Superiority.

That independent acts should conform to the strategy and military stance chosen by a nation in pursuit of its political aims is important not only with respect to the once-for-all restructuring of forces and their deployment. It is also important with respect to day to day decisions over the development and acquisition of weapons, the training and deployment of forces and everything else that goes to make up doctrine.

The next question to consider is how to influence your neighbour in a direction that positively helps you achieve your defensive objectives.

Country A, having taken unilateral steps towards non-nuclear defensiveness and nuclear Sufficiency, will wish to induce B to move in the same direction. For this purpose A can engage in discussion, as we have defined it here, with the object of persuading B that, if his political aims are peaceful, it is in his interest too to change his military stance to nuclear Sufficiency and non-nuclear Defensive Superiority so as to improve stability and ease the confrontation between them. The argument that a combined change in strategy will reduce the risk of pre-emptive attack may be invoked but it will have less force when applied to the second of two countries to make the change than to the first. For if one has made the change and reduced its capacity to attack, the *mutual* fear that, if I do not attack him first, he will attack me for fear I will attack him, will have been reduced.

If country B cannot be persuaded to move in sympathy with A, there seems little that A can do other than continue discussion, hoping that one day it will bear fruit. Meanwhile it should go as far as it prudently can in the implementation by independent actions of the strategic stance of nuclear Sufficiency and non-nuclear Defensive Superiority.

The question remains, when is negotiation needed? It will be needed insofar as the two sides confront each other with forces that are threatening to each other's security and those forces cannot, consistently with stability and economy, be removed unilaterally or replaced by defences.

Two criteria suggest themselves. First, are the offensive characteristics of the forces such that they cannot be neutralised by any defensive move?

At the non-nuclear level, chemical weapons are a category which comes to mind. The move to a defensive stance that one country in a confrontation could take would be to get rid of chemical weapons and concentrate on protective measures. But it may be the case – though this is open to debate – that protective measures cannot be reckoned as more than a weak substitute for an offensive capability that provides a threat of retaliation and so deters the use of chemical weapons by your opponent. Therefore reciprocity, and hence negotiation, are needed.

Another category of weapon to which the same argument applies is aircaft. They may be used to attack one another's airfields, and defences against them are of uncertain effectiveness. For one side to dispense with them may therefore be considered too risky.

At the nuclear level, the same argument applies. If your aims are peaceful, you should go for Sufficiency, as defined earlier, and you should not threaten or obstruct your opponent's nuclear weapons since to do so will be destabilising, i.e. it will make him less secure and cause him to arm more. If you start from a position where you and your opponent possess destabilising systems, you will increase your security – and his – by reducing the risk of pre-emptive attack if you remove those systems unilaterally, so long as you preserve Sufficiency, e.g. through the possession of invulnerable submarine-launched missiles. There are no grounds for demanding reciprocity through negotiation so long as Sufficiency is possessed, but there is a case for urging him to follow by means of consultation. Negotiation would become necessary in two sets of circumstances, analogous to the circumstances of chemical weapons discussed above:

(a) If you wished to go below Sufficiency and get rid of nuclear weapons, but, because of continuing mistrust, you were not willing unilaterally to join the states which do without them and you therefore sought reciprocity.

(b) If the only systems possessed by and available to both sides were so unstable (e.g. land-based missiles many times MIRVed) that neither side felt it could de-MIRV unilaterally without excessive risk of one-sided vulnerability to a disarming first strike.

The second criterion for deciding when negotiation is needed is whether the forces under consideration have a considerable defensive as well as offensive capability, so that their removal by one side will deprive it of defensive as well as offensive strength, possibly giving the other side both offensive superiority and defensive superiority. Mobile armoured forces are an example.

THE PRIMACY OF STRATEGY

These criteria may overlap, and there will constantly be the question whether it is necessary to negotiate or whether you can rely on discussion and independent action promoted by discussion. What matters is that the three methods should be used in harmony. For that to happen, strategy must be coherent and effectively enforced.

Strategy is supreme; independent actions, consultation and negotiation are methods of implementing its dictates. If strategy is not coherent the three methods are unlikely to be used in harmony, and it will consequently be difficult to make progress. If strategy is coherent and it is vigorously applied, it should follow that a nation (or alliance) in a nuclear setting, having adopted a non-nuclear stance of Defensive Superiority and nuclear stance of Sufficiency, would go as far as it safely could to reduce by independent action its present and future offensive capabilities; that it would engage in Consultation with the other side about how to move together towards those objectives; and, where it was necessary according to the criteria indicated above, it would negotiate the limitation or elimination of selected offensive non-nuclear forces and excessive nuclear forces. This implies that arms negotiations should be approached in a very different way from that which has been customary in the Cold War.

THE OBJECTIVES OF NEGOTIATION

Arms negotiations, which have been pursued with interruptions for nearly 100 years, have been and still are based on the belief that the way to achieve security and check or reverse an arms race is to seek balanced limits to arms. The main exception is the short period in 1932–33 when qualitative disarmament was pursued. (A short history of arms negotiations since 1899 is given in an Appendix.)

The idea that you need balance has rested on the notion that the way to keep the peace is to maintain a balance of arms *vis-à-vis* your potential opponent. This in turn rests on the seductively simple idea that if your opponent is stronger than you, he will be able to defeat you; therefore to defend yourself you must keep up with him in arms; you must be as strong as he is, or stronger; you must pursue balance in arms for the sake of security. And this idea rests on the implicit assumption that all forces have an offensive capability as great as, or greater than, their defensive capability.

In the inter-war years, when disarmament negotiations were between many nations of different sizes which were not bound together in alliances but were weakly committed to collective security, quotas for countries were discussed, based on population and other factors; and the objective, which was then discussed, was complete disarmament, right down to zero other than forces for internal law and order. In the post-war period, when the main competition in arms has been between two blocks, the notion of balance has been invoked in its simple bilateral sense.

The theoretical objections to the pursuit of balance were stated in Chapter 2. Briefly, the argument for pursuing balance rests on the assumption that forces are offensive, but offensiveness also means that balance is an unstable condition.

The two classic models of an arms race – Richardson's model and 'Prisoner's Dilemma' (an application of Game Theory) take no account of these fundamental qualifications to the notion that the pursuit of balance produces security. Both models rest implicitly on the assumption that there exist only all-round forces, equally suitable for the purpose of defence or offence, and on the assumption that there is no saturation point beyond which the acquisition of more nuclear weapons or other weapons of extreme destructiveness is futile. Richardson's model usefully demonstrates that where those assumptions hold and there is mistrust (which arms themselves may cause), arming is an unstable process and arms levels will go upwards, moderated, he assumed, only by reluctance to spend more. Prisoner's Dilemma demonstrates that if superiority in arms brings political gains (through war or threat of war) to the winner at the expense of the loser, and you cannot trust your armed neighbour to abide by a deal in which you both agree to reduce arms, it will pay to keep your arms rather than make a deal and risk being double-crossed. These results are the reasonable and inevitable consequence of the assumption that the same forces are suitable for offence and defence and the assumption that there is no saturation point – and the assumption that there are gains to be made from war or threat of war.

These models represent what has happened in the past rather well, but they may have done harm by inculcating the notion that one must accept that the world is bound still to be like this today. The models have been used extensively in the teaching of international relations, arms control, strategy and peace research.

The practical objections to the pursuit of balance are no less compelling. They concern asymmetry and misperception.

Even if information was complete, a balance of military strength between two nations could be defined *precisely* only if the two nations were symmetrical – if they had the same weapons, the same sized armies, navies and air forces, with men of the same age, training and morale; the same arms industries, the same geography and the same allies (or none); and so on. Only if the conditions of symmetry were fulfilled, to the point where two states (or alliances) were *identical*, could we declare without risk of contradiction that there was a precise military balance. If there are asymmetries, if for example there are differences in weapons and in the period of training of the forces of two nations, there is no precise way of measuring those differences and reducing them to a common mathematical unit of 'strength' so as to arrive at a precise answer to the effect that, on balance, A is stronger than B. In the language of the economist, there is no set of weights that one can observe, let alone use without dispute, to combine into a single aggregate measure the disparate variables that make up military strength.

In practice, nothing is symmetrical. There is no possibility of precise measurement of the balance of strength. Added to which, information is incomplete and uncertain, partly because intelligence is imperfect, partly because some things cannot be known: you cannot know how your potential opponent's forces, or your own, will perform in the event of war; and you cannot have sure information about future strength, which is what must guide your decisions to acquire new weapons and forces. You have to rely on predictive judgement which will often be wrong – how often is indicated by the inability of military experts to predict the outcome of wars: if the military balance could be measured, we could predict who would win.[2]

The second problem is that in the exercise of judgement biased perception comes in. Each analyst or journalist who attempts to judge the balance and advise politicians and the public about it must decide what variables to select, what interpretation to put on the data for each and their relative importance. Each politician or member of the public who looks at what the analysts and journalists have to offer must decide which of them to follow and what interpretation to put on his work. Alarmists will pick on the analysts whose work suggests the opponent is stronger. Escapists will pick on the analysts whose work suggests the opposite. In one period, escapism may prevail: the 1930s are an example. In another, alarmism will prevail: the post-war arms race is an example.

Even if there is nothing you could call alarmism, only caution, the pursuit of balance is enough to generate and perpetuate an arms race. The cautious man, following the precept that balance brings security, which carries with it the notion that too little is dangerous and too much adds to safety, will over-insure in the acquisition of arms and in the negotiation of arms limitations. But if only one of two opposed nations does that, the result will be an arms race and deadlock in negotiation. The side that tries to get ahead forces the other to race in pursuit of balance and to resist the unbalanced arms proposals it puts forward. The acquisition of more arms and the negotiation of arms limits will be two parts of the pursuit of balance as the rival nations seek to limit categories of arms in which the other side has an advantage and to develop more weapons outside the categories to which limits apply.

Since asymmetries abound and the arguments about balance can never be resolved, it is predictable that 'racing while talking' will continue until balance is abandoned as the criterion of security and stability.

The necessary condition for the abandonment of the pursuit of balance is a change in strategy. So long as strategy is such that forces are sought which have an offensive capability as great as, or greater than, their defensive capability, it follows that:

(a)   balance or, to err on the safe side, superiority will be sought;
(b)   there will be little or no place for positive dialogue, in the form of Consultation, between the two sides; and
(c)   negotiation will be an adversarial process in which both sides will seek relative strength.

Once strategy is made consistent with peaceful aims and the pursuit of rapprochement, it follows that:

(a)   in place of balance, non-nuclear Defensive Superiority and nuclear Sufficiency become the military stances to pursue;
(b)   there is a place for positive dialogue, in the form of Consultation, about how to achieve common objectives; and
(c)   negotiation can cease to be an adversarial pursuit of relative strength and can become a cooperative pursuit of nuclear Sufficiency and Mutual Defensive Superiority.

The last point requires elaboration. If the military stance you are pursuing at the nuclear level is Sufficiency, there is no need to worry about changes in the other side's nuclear arsenal so long as it does not threaten your Sufficiency; and your strategy does not require you to acquire nuclear forces that threaten the other side's nuclear forces: on the contrary, your strategy will tell you that you should refrain from such action since it causes instability and negative feedback.

Similarly at the non-nuclear level, if you adopt a defensive strategy and seek Mutual Defensive Superiority, your strategy will not tell you to pursue relative offensive strength. Rather it will tell you to get rid of offensive strength and maximise defensive strength on both sides. Negotiation is an aspect of strategy, a means of implementing strategy. The key to progress in the introduction of a change of strategy does not lie in putting effort into negotiation as we know it; it lies in changing the strategies from which negotiation derives and gets its guidance.

OBSTACLES TO CHANGE

The abandonment of strategies that emphasise offensive strength, and their corollary, the pursuit of balance in arms, is not likely to come about easily. In addition to the usual institutional resistance to change, there are two particular problems.

As was noted earlier, there can be geo-political conditions where a direct switch to defensive policies presents problems – the 'strong country in the middle' problem (Chapter 2) and the problem of the small country with no depth, for example, Israel.

Secondly, there are arguments which suggest that the military may be resistant to the abandonment of the offensive in favour of the defensive. Military officers, in the words of Bernard Brodie, 'are trained to be biased in favour of the offensive, much as ordinary people are trained to be biased in favour of virtue. Aggressiveness in a commander is considered a great merit, and history suggests that it should be so.[3]

Five reasons why the military favour the offensive are offered by Sagan:

1. Offensive doctrines enhance the power and the size of military organisations because larger and more expensive forces, are required for offence than defence.
2. Offensive doctrines promote military autonomy.
3. Offensives enhance the prestige and self-image of military officers, in contrast to defensive operations which may be seen as passive and less glorious.
4. The offensive permits you to take the initiative which, according to a very old argument, permits you to conduct a battle, at least in its early stages, according to your plan.

5.   Military planning, which requires you to work up a vision of a hostile enemy and a likelihood of war, leads military men to favour 'preventive wars and preemptive strikes when necessary and decisive operations when possible'.[4]

From statements of this kind it is easy to form the view that a bias towards the offensive is generally inevitable. But the matter is not as simple as that. The inculcation of a fighting spirit, which means a readiness to kill and an eagerness to knock out your opponent before he knocks you out, is essential in the training of a recruit to be a fighting man and in the training of small groups at the tactical level. But that does not mean that *strategy* has to be offensive. A fighting spirit can be combined with a defensive strategy if peaceful political aims are built into the formulation of strategy. For example, the Swedes, Swiss and Yugoslavs appear to possess a vigorous fighting spirit that would be unleashed if their countries were attacked, yet their strategies are not offensive. The trouble is that where the size and circumstances of a nation are such that there is no compelling political reason why its national aims and strategy should be defensive, the glorification of the offensive spirit can easily be carried over from individual conduct and tactical training into strategy and thence into images of an heroic role for the nation which are translated into political aims.

Sagan implies that the military will resist the renunciation of the offensive because they will sense that to go defensive, and seek to induce their potential opponents to go defensive, is a policy which, if successful, will remove their *raison d'être*. But if that is so, why do the military of non-aligned nations in Europe not resist defensiveness on these grounds. The explanation may be partly that their permanent military establishment is small, since they rely so heavily on conscripts and reserves. Another explanation is that, since these non-aligned countries are peripheral to the confrontation in Europe, whether their strategy and forces are defensive or offensive has made little or no difference to the risks of a European war, and hence to their *raison d'être*. It is the big powers, the leading members of the alliances, that have the largest regular military establishments in relation to population, and it is their policies that primarily determine whether there is confrontation and military competition or not.

In any event, it would be wrong generally to accuse the military of inflexibility and a love of the offensive at the strategic level. It is from serving or retired members of the armed forces that heretical ideas have often come, for example, Fuller, Liddell Hart, de Gaulle and Tukhachevsky with the idea of mobile armoured warfare; and Liddell Hart, von Bonin, Brossollet, Löser, Schmähling and Spannocchi with the idea of defensive defence. In this essay I am indeed expounding and putting into a general theoretical framework ideas that mostly come from military officers.

It may well be that a change from offensiveness is likely to be resisted most strongly by those in the weapons industry, the weapons laboratories and the think-tanks who have come to live by the notion that the constant development of new threatening weapons is the way to contribute to security and to the standing of the nation. In the West, this community, in contrast to military, seems to have produced few heretics who advocate a change in strategy.

OFFENSIVE AIMS

If a nation's political aims are offensive, meaning that it aims to attack or to threaten to attack, its appropriate actions are very different and rather limited.

Whether it declares its aims publicly, as Hitler did, or claims that its aims are peaceful, its arms policy will be directed at acquiring the requisite non-nuclear Offensive Superiority and perhaps nuclear Supremacy. In consultations, it may seek to calm its opponent. As regards negotiations, a government may walk out as part of a militaristic stance intended to intimidate its opponents and potential neutrals and to rouse its population at home; or it may play along, seeking to lull its opponent and gain advantage thereby. It is not obvious which tactic is better, nor that either will make much difference.

If the political aim of a nation is offensive in the more limited sense of seeking not to attack its neighbour but to strain his politico–economic system by forcing him into an arms race, it will be necessary for it to adopt a strategy and force posture sufficiently offensive to create in the neighbour's mind the fear that he may be attacked.

6 Interpretation of the Period since 1945

The next step is to apply our theoretical approach to the central confrontation between the nuclear powers since 1945. We shall look at the military strategies followed by each side at the nuclear and non-nuclear levels. We shall not attempt to explain the political and economic forces which influenced the choice of policies. We seek only to see what were the dominant arguments and thrusts of policy. But the processes beneath the surface should not be forgotten.

MILITARY DOCTRINE

A military doctrine built around offensive use was inevitable at the nuclear level because nuclear weapons are so destructive that they can be used only to attack or threaten attack.

That offensive doctrines – or at least the absence of defensive doctrine – should have dominated the sub-nuclear level of strategic thinking was not inevitable. Yet that was the case until recently when, under Mr Gorbachev, the Soviet Union and the WTO declared that they were adopting a defensive doctrine and had started on its implementation.

The persistence of offensive doctrines can in part be attributed to some general reasons which probably influenced both sides.

First, there is the normal and understandable tendency of the military, for the reasons discussed earlier, to be predisposed to the offensive as a way of fighting (Chapter 5).

Secondly, ideas about how to use nuclear threats to keep your potential enemy at bay with nuclear forces spilled over into thinking about non-nuclear forces. The same language was used. In the West, the word deterrence came to be used interchangeably with the word defence and quite commonly displaced it, although they have different meanings. To deter, derived from the Latin word *terrere*, means to prevent by fear, to threaten retaliation; to defend, derived from *fendere*, means to fend off, to deny possession.

Thirdly, the Second World War saw the triumph of mobile warfare with its emphasis of surprise attack, on defensive–offensive actions and on the pursuit of decisive victory. All the armies now in Europe are the 'children of Hitler's tank armies, designed for attack and blitzkrieg'. In the war, both the Red Army and the United States and allied armies in Europe had to equip and train themselves for attack, since their task was to liberate occupied Europe. Since then the structure of the armies has not changed. 'Each weapon system has been modernised, with new tanks replacing old ones, and becoming two or three times more expensive: but there has been no change in the conventional force structure' which remains one that 'gives the decisive advantage to the attacking side – which is not surprising since it was for this purpose that the structure was developed'.[1] The military on both sides carried forward this notion of how war can most successfully be fought.

Apart from these general reasons, there were particular features of the strategic situation at the end of the war which contributed to the adoption of offensiveness. The Soviet Union and the western allies mistrusted each other. The main ingredients of their mutual mistrust were the conflict in ideology between revolutionary communism and capitalism, the memory on both sides of the occasions when the other side did a deal with Hitler, and the experience of the war when cooperation in pursuit of military victory was tainted by mistrust over long-term political objectives. On top of this, the United States had developed the atomic bomb, had used it and had shown that it sought not to share it with the Soviet Union. On the other side, the Soviet Union kept large armies in eastern Europe while the West demobilised. The basic military equation was that the American bomb and the large Soviet army offset each other; the threat of an American nuclear attack matched the threat of Soviet invasion of western Europe and *vice versa*. This relationship was to be crystallised on the American side in the doctrine of massive nuclear retaliation and on the Soviet side in a doctrine for non-nuclear forces which could equally well have been called massive retaliation. In both cases, the powerful offensive forces which went with the doctrine could be interpreted by a worst-case analyst, or indeed a cautious analyst, as evidence of aggressive intentions.

SOVIET AND WTO NON-NUCLEAR DOCTRINE

The WTO grew as a highly integrated structure under Soviet leadership, as regards command, equipment, training and other military matters. Soviet doctrine, which is discussed in the Soviet military press and closely followed in the West, is therefore what we need to look at.

In the Soviet Union, the attention given to military doctrine is of a different order and kind from the attention given to it in other countries. The desirability of a unified military doctrine had been a theme in pre-Revolutionary military thought in Russia, and there was a lively debate before 1914.[2] After the Revolution and the Civil War, the formulation of doctrine became a central element in a complex set of struggles over military matters in which the main factions and individuals seeking power took positions on ideology and on technical and military points. The achievement of a statement of military doctrines seems to have been rather like the achievement of a statement of religious doctrine within a warring church: 'The debates on doctrine, in which the Soviet command had entered, embraced a very wide field, the intrinsic issues being complicated by the fact that many of the arguments were only a very thin screen for personal or group ambitions.'[3]

That this was so is understandable. The normal continuity of military thought and practice was broken by Russia's defeat in the 1914-18 war and by the Revolution. Moreover, the experience of the Civil War was of questionable relevance to the strategy needed by the new Soviet state facing a hostile world – though its relevance was one point at issue. The political cross-currents which impinged on military doctrine included the struggle for power between Stalin and Trotsky; arguments over the role of ex-imperial officers, who had expertise, versus Revolutionary heroes; argument over a professional army versus a people's militia; arguments over the relative power of political commissars versus military officers; and then there were the trials of the late 1930s, when, to diminish the power of the armed forces, Stalin liquidated many of the leaders of the Soviet military and a large part of the officer corps.

The dangers of 'military doctrinairism', meaning dogmatic insistence upon certain arbitrarily selected principles, were pointed out by Trotsky, but his view was treated as heresy.[4] The issue which concerns us here – the relative role assigned to defence and offence – was at the centre of discussions of doctrine.

Although the Soviet Union's military aims became defensive once 'Socialism in One State' was adopted, and although in the 1930s she was increasingly on the defensive, fearful of attack as Japan and Germany gathered strength, there was a failure to adopt an effective defensive doctrine. In all the political turmoil of the period, there were many reasons for this failure but one was the persistent emphasis on the offensive. Indeed, the offensive seems to have been extolled to the point where one could speak of a cult of the offensive similar to that in France before 1914. The offensive was stressed as a peculiarly proletarian principle;[5] and it has been suggested that 'This strong preference for activity and the offensive is probably in part an (unrecognised) psychologically defensive manifestation induced by fear', analogous to the aggression of a person with a 'chip on his shoulder'.[6]

Whatever its causes, the emphasis on the offensive, together with the disbanding of the mechanised corps built up by Tukhachevsky, are two of the leading explanations offered for the defeats suffered by the Red Army when the Germans attacked in June 1941.

In the words of a British military historian commenting on the defeat of the Red Army in the face of the German attack in 1941:

> the Red Army needed drastically new defensive tactics, instead of just stringing out men and guns (in particular the tanks) uniformly along the front. More than that, however, the whole notion of the Red Army as an undifferentiated mass offensive instrument required overhauling.[7]

And in the words of a Soviet military writer (General Vorob'ev), 'the undue emphasis on the offensive' and 'carrying the war into the enemy's territory' was the factor which hampered proper defensive enemy's territory' was the factor which hampered proper defensive planning.[8]

The evolution of Soviet doctrine after the war differed from that in the West in two related respects.

First, whereas in the West, which initially had a nuclear monopoly, nuclear doctrine evolved round nuclear weapons as a new and separate type of weapon, in the Soviet Union nuclear weapons, which came later, were regarded as additions to the non-nuclear forces which were bound to be used alongside non-nuclear forces.

Secondly, whereas the West pursued deterrence, meaning the idea of avoiding war by deploying and threatening retaliation with nuclear weapons, superimposed on a layer of non-nuclear forces, the Soviet Union was concerned with planning how to win a war should it occur.

These differences can be explained by the geography and history of the confrontation. The United States, with no hostile nations on its home frontiers, did not face the possibility that its homeland would be attacked by non-nuclear forces; it was concerned to prevent military action far afield and, having started with a nuclear monopoly, it had acquired the habit of threatening in general terms the use of nuclear weapons. On the other hand, the Soviet Union was encircled – a condition resulting from the West's policy of containment – and if war occurred the Soviet Union would be occupied if it lost: classical military logic said that the way to avoid that outcome was to plan to conquer the enemy's forces should he attack you, if necessary over-running the territory from which they came. And since the United States had nuclear weapons first and threatened to use them, it is understandable that the Soviet Union should have made its plans on the assumption that they would be used.

These points, together with the post-revolutionary emphasis on the offensive, alone help to explain why the Soviet Union adopted a non-nuclear doctrine with strong emphasis on the offensive. But from eastern and western sources there are other explanations on offer, so many that it can be said that the Soviet's offensive non-nuclear stance has been over-explained. It is impossible to know the validity or relative importance of the following explanations:

1. An explanation already noted: before the Soviet Union acquired a nuclear armoury in which it felt confident, it sought to threaten Western Europe with non-nuclear forces as a counter to the nuclear threat posed by the United States, a policy that was carried on by inertia.[9]

2. The terrain of the Soviet Union with its huge empty spaces and lack of defensive barriers was such that it was found in the Second World War, and before, that it was not generally possible to rely for defence on dispersed forces with low mobility. It was necessary to rely mainly on mobile armoured forces capable of manoeuvring to meet the enemy at the point where he massed his forces and attacked and then going over to the offensive to drive him out. The defence, which had been neglected before the war, was found to be a highly important part of offensive operations, for example, as part of encirclement or as an accompaniment to an attack at another point. But the strong emphasis in operational doctrine was on the offensive.

3. The opening phases of the war, when the Soviet Union suffered humiliating defeats, were regarded as a failure in defence and the later phases as a success for the offensive. The success was

glorified, and the failure, upon which it was not judicious to dwell, was not subjected to searching analysis.

4. The Soviet military in making plans for a war which did not go nuclear – a contingency that their planners were bound to provide for and which they may have considered more likely once the Soviet Union had nuclear strength – saw that they must plan to sweep swiftly to the Atlantic so as to seize the ports before the United States could land reinforcements and bring its huge potential resources to bear in Europe, as it had done in the two world wars.[10]

5. After its appalling experience in the Second World War, the Soviet Union was determined to prevent war flowing onto Soviet soil again. And it planned to keep the enemy out of the territory of its colonies in eastern Europe whose peoples might take the wrong side given a chance.

Unlike NATO, the Soviet Union has never had a declared policy of first use of nuclear weapons. That can be attributed to its strength in non-nuclear forces and initial relative weakness in nuclear forces, or to prudence, or to considerations of presentation rather than substance: what a nation says about when it will use nuclear weapons does not determine what it can do.

Whatever the true cause, or combination of causes, of the Soviet Union's post-war non-nuclear doctrine (meaning, let it be clear, its doctrine as to *how* it has planned to fight *if* war broke out, not whether it would start a war) the fact that the doctrine was offensive has been conceded by Soviet experts recently when they have been arguing the case for their new defensive doctrine for non-nuclear forces. Thus Alexei Arbatov, a leading Soviet defence analyst, has written in the new 'Yearbook on Disarmament and Security', produced by one of the top research institutes in Moscow, as follows:

The following thesis served as the point of departure in the past: foreign policy should in every way contribute to the prevention of war and the strengthening of peace, however, if a war were unleashed against the USSR and its allies, their armed forces should have the capability necessary for crushing the enemy, primarily including the waging of resolute offensive operations at all levels of the conflict. The greater the capacity for such operations, the stronger the defense, the more reliable the deterrence of hostile actions of the other side, and the better the conditions for the maintenance of peace. This logic was expressed in many works, including statements and publications by Soviet military experts.[11]

Alexei Arbatov goes on to say that this policy caused negative feedback in the West, where it was read as evidence of offensive intentions and aggravated the arms race and political tension.

UNITED STATES/NATO NON-NUCLEAR DOCTRINE

When, in the face of the perceived Soviet military threat, the parties to the North Atlantic Treaty of 1949 agreed, in 1950, to create NATO, a military organisation ready to fight, they largely resurrected the structure of the Allied forces under American command which had liberated Western Europe. The same kind of forces were called for; the same supreme commander, General Eisenhower, was put in charge.[12] Nuclear weapons existed in small numbers as an ultimate weapon. United States forces were in Europe occupying part of Germany; and United States aircraft potentially capable of carrying nuclear weapons were brought to Britain during the Berlin Blockade in 1948 and stayed on. The threat that nuclear weapons might be used emanated from their very existence and deployment. Nevertheless the initial NATO plan, set out in February 1952 in the Lisbon force goals, called for enough NATO divisions to be able to hold a Soviet attack – about 100 divisions, or roughly the same number as there were on the western front at the end of the war – though they were now to consist mostly of reservists who had served in the war. The Lisbon force goals should perhaps be called a manifesto rather than a plan. They derived from an exercise in persuasion in which the United States sought to induce the European nations to contribute more forces and offered aid. But, as the word goals implies, the members, rather than commit themselves to raise the divisions declared to be necessary, were willing only to utter a collective exhortation to themselves.

With Germany allowed neither to contribute to defence nor to have a say in military plans, NATO military planning was based on the strategy of falling back on the natural barrier of the Rhine, trading German territory for time and making the Rhine the main line of resistance.

The Lisbon force goals were never approximately met, partly because the fear of a Soviet attack on Europe caused by the attack on South Korea faded quickly, partly because the idea of matching the Soviets' estimated 175 divisions looked hopeless. Not only was there still argument about how and on what scale Germany should contribute military forces to NATO, but Britain and France, with their economies still recovering from the war, had part of their forces committed to the residue of their empires.

NATO moved to a policy of explicit and immediate reliance on nuclear weapons. This followed not just from the refusal of the members to increase their conventional forces in Europe but also from the new policy of placing much greater reliance on nuclear weapons introduced by General Eisenhower after he became President at the beginning of 1953. He told the United States Chiefs of Staff that they could plan to use nuclear weapons of all shapes and sizes in the future wherever this would work to the advantage of the United States.[13] His decision has been attributed to such things as the domestic reaction to the Korean conflict, the continued faith in the efficacy of air power, a desire for budgetary economy, and the American desire for simple solutions.[14] This was the era when the United States threatened massive nuclear retaliation against aggression anywhere in the world.

NATO adopted the new strategy in two bites. In December 1954, it accepted the American New Look, meaning that as a basis for planning nuclear weapons should be used as if they were conventional weapons; and then in December 1956 it formally adopted, in a document known as MC 14/2, the doctrine of Massive Retaliation.

The question how in practice to combine nuclear weapons, which now included weapons of smaller yield than before, with the use of other forces was apparently met with three main suggestions: their use at a river crossing where invading troops were massed; the dispersion of defending forces into well-protected static positions from which they would direct nuclear weapons at enemy forces in the areas in between; and nuclear attacks on Soviet bases and cities followed by airborne landings to liberate the supposedly welcoming people.[15]

Although the apparent cheapness of nuclear defence was attractive, doubts about the strategy were felt from an early stage, principally in the United States where it was questioned whether it was prudent for the United States to have little or no alternative, when faced by a conflict overseas (and there is no risk of a major conflict at its own frontiers), but to use nuclear weapons, thereby risking nuclear retaliation against the United States homeland, or give way. The growth in Soviet nuclear strength contributed to this feeling, as did the discovery by the Kennedy administration in the Berlin crisis of 1961 that there was a paucity of plans that did not rely on the early use of nuclear weapons.[16]

War games had shown that the use of tactical nuclear weapons meant the nuclear annihilation of the area that was meant to be defended. In Germany, which was now a substantial contributor to the military strength of NATO, having been admitted to membership in 1955, there was understandable unease about being made a nuclear battlefield; and France had withdrawn from NATO (though not from the North Atlantic Alliance)[17] rather than be subject to United States nuclear decisions.

Under President Kennedy and Secretary of Defense McNamara, the United States sought to escape from the doctrine of Massive Retaliation, with its all or nothing choices, by developing a capacity to wage limited war, meaning war without resort to nuclear weapons – or 'sub-nuclear war'. In NATO it proposed to the other members that there should be more non-nuclear forces and less reliance on nuclear forces. The outcome, after years of argument in NATO was the adoption in May 1967 of the doctrine of Flexible Response.

The doctrine is a compromise, achieved by ambiguity, between a mesh of conflicting views. The two main strands were the United States' desire to reduce reliance on nuclear weapons so as to reduce the risk that the United States might be blown up and, on the other hand, a European desire to have United States nuclear 'protection' reaffirmed and yet minimise the risk that nuclear weapons would be used. A further justification for ambiguity is the well-known proposition that you must generate uncertainty: you must *not* say that you will use nuclear weapons when an invader has advanced 100 miles since to do so is to encourage your neighbour to try taking a slice of territory 99 miles deep, or less.

In essence, Flexible Response is a qualified, toned down version of Massive Retaliation. Instead of suggesting that nuclear weapons will be used as soon as any non-nuclear battle is joined, it says that NATO will first try non-nuclear defence and will use nuclear weapons if the non-nuclear defence is failing; it suggests that escalation may start with limited use of theatre nuclear weapons rather than all-out use of nuclear weapons, including those in the United States; but it emphasises that all-out use is the ultimate threat.

The difference between Massive Retaliation and Flexible Response has been less than it might have been because of two political constraints on the non-nuclear strategy that could be adopted. Both are there at the insistence of West Germany.

First, there is the commitment to 'forward defence', meaning the defence of the frontiers of West Germany. Understandably, the West German Government, when it rearmed and began to make a substantial contribution to NATO, asked that a doctrine based on defending its territory at the frontier should replace the old NATO doctrine of falling back on the Rhine and letting Germany be taken by the attacker. The doctrine of Massive Retaliation, which threatened massive retaliation if frontiers were breached, had met that desideratum. When, in negotiation, Massive Retaliation was being replaced by Flexible Response, something had to be put in its place to reassure Bonn that NATO would not again plan to surrender German territory. For this purpose, NATO, in September 1963, officially adopted a commitment to Forward Defence, meaning that forces should be deployed forward and should attempt to defend West Germany from the frontier.[18]

The second political constraint on NATO non-nuclear strategy has been the refusal of West Germany to allow the construction of prepared defences in the form of fortifications, earthworks or even militarily-useful afforestation or landscaping, on the grounds that their introduction would confirm in an unacceptable degree the political division of Germany. (There is, I understand, a similar lack of defensive works on the eastern side of the line that divides NATO and the WTO.)

These two constraints mean that fighting must take place forward yet without one of the main benefits of being a defender – prepared positions – a point about which the West German military have been known to complain bitterly in private. The result has been to reinforce the tendency of NATO to stick to the inherited tradition of mobile warfare as a means of non-nuclear defence, leading if necessary to use of nuclear weapons – and to make that strategy more risky than it might otherwise be.

At the end of the 1970s there appeared to be some signs of a possible shift, led by the British army, towards greater reliance on non-mechanised infantry organised into defensive anti-tank positions around the villages and around the towns that have become much more numerous in Germany since the war and offer good settings for defence. The scheme was derived from the methods used successfully by the German army against the British armoured forces in Normandy in 1944. These, and similar ideas generated in other armies, were discussed at a conference of NATO officers on the employment of non-mechanised infantry in Hamburg in 1980.[19] Since then, however, there has been renewed emphasis on the acquisition of forces with offensive characteristics so as to have a greater capability for counter-offensive operations.

Two new notions were generated in the United States – Air-Land Battle and Deep Strike. Both are based on new technologies. The first, which has been adopted by the United States Army generally, is a method of swift deep attack using airborne forces and helicopters in combination with mobile armoured ground forces. The second – Deep Strike – was designed specifically for NATO and consists in the use of accurate missiles to strike at 'rich' targets far behind the lines, for example, headquarters, choke points in lines of communication and concentrated forces.

These American doctrines have not been adopted as such by NATO, where there are in any case variations in non-nuclear doctrine from one country to another, but the idea of modernising and strengthening NATO's capability for deep strikes against the WTO second echelon forces, which would need to be brought forward to take part in an attack on NATO, has been adopted as the FOFA Concept, where FOFA stands for follow-on forces attack; and the NATO military leadership has continued to advocate investment in armoured and mechanised forces with the characteristics of firepower, mobility and speed so as to be able, in the words of the Supreme Commander, to conduct 'defensive manoeuvre operations designed to seize the initiative from the attacker and turn it to the advantage of the defender'.[20]

The Soviet Union and WTO have expressed concern at the potential capacity of FOFA to cripple their forces. A further point of concern is that the new long-range weapons, like the aircraft that are their precursors, are dual purpose, i.e. can be used with nuclear or non-nuclear warheads, a characteristic which aggravates the problems of specifying and verifying any negotiated limits on nuclear weapons.

NATO has always taken the line that its intentions are defensive and that, since its non-nuclear forces are smaller than those of the WTO, there can be no question of them posing a threat to the WTO; that the forces are designed for mobile armoured warfare and for deep strikes to incapacitate the WTO is immaterial.

There can be no doubt that NATO's non-nuclear strategy is at odds with the pursuit of defensiveness and stability and will become increasingly inconsistent with stability if, as NATO demands, the offensive forces of the WTO and NATO are reduced by asymmetric cuts to equality.

NATO doctrine has been dominated by the United States, the most powerful member and the first nuclear power. The influence of other European members, particularly West Germany, has increased since the early post-war years and might have increased further as their economic strength grew relative to that of the United States, but they have not taken two steps that would have made them less dependent on the United States: they have not increased their non-nuclear forces (though they have gone a long way) and changed their strategy in such a way that they have less need, or no need, of United States non-nuclear forces in Europe; nor have they shown a clear desire to establish a European nuclear force, let alone taken all the steps towards political unity which would be required by that policy. Apart from anything else, to remain dependent on the United States has been both economical and reassuring compared with breaking away; there has been a nervous desire to keep the United States committed to Europe.

So far the discussion in this chapter has been concerned with the overall doctrine of both sides and with the doctrine for non-nuclear forces, insofar as it can be isolated. We turn to nuclear policies.

NUCLEAR DOCTRINE

As we have seen in Chapters 2 and 3, once each of two opposed nations has enough nuclear weapons to cause unacceptable death and destruction to the other, the strategy consistent with peaceful aims is not to accumulate more weapons but to accept Sufficiency as an objective and try to resolve the international differences by political means. If aims are offensive there is, in theory, the alternative of seeking Supremacy, meaning a monopoly or near monopoly achieved by acquiring a capability to knock out or intercept your opponent's nuclear weapons, but that is not a realistic alternative once your opponent has a significant nuclear capability and can react to whatever you do by acquiring more nuclear weapons or by introducing other counter-measures. In between these two policies, there is the no man's land where nations may seek relative nuclear strength in the hopes that, although unusable, it will yield political gains, or with the object of increasing the risks of war in the paradoxical belief that that is a good way to avoid war; or they may be driven simply by domestic political pressures generated by the arms race.

As a starting point, let us ask what would be a Sufficiency of nuclear weapons, meaning a number sufficient to cause unacceptable death and destruction to another nation and so deter its political leaders, by threat of retaliation. It is natural to start by thinking of Hiroshima and Nagasaki: twice a small weapon was used with devastating effect; and of Chernobyl, where something like a nuclear weapon went off though it produced only fall-out: the direct casualties from explosion or burns were negligible; and one will think of the fear generated by the notion that a nuclear weapon might come into the hands of Colonel Gadaffi, a man who, it seems to be believed, might really use one if he had one. These are the most relevant bits of evidence to go by, for something happened, or really might happen, of the kind we are attempting to think about.

The conclusion to which a person who thinks along these lines is likely to be led is that the prospect that one modern nuclear weapon might hit a city is very probably enough to dissuade a political leader from military adventure; ten weapons on ten cities would be such an appalling catastrophe that if it did not deter our hypothetical leader it is hard to think what would; to go for 100 weapons would be a tenfold act of over-insurance and surely should be sufficient to satisfy anyone.[21]

That both sides went far beyond Sufficiency and yet have achieved a stalemate rather than anything remotely resembling Supremacy is clear: each side possesses about 25,000 warheads. It is also clear that this has been the result of a competitive process – an arms race – driven by a complex of economic, technical and political forces within the Soviet Union and the United States, as well as by interaction between the two nations. On the United States side one can see that there has been competition between researchers, weapons makers, politicians, political parties and interest groups, including the rival armed services; and one can see that from the beginning of the nuclear arms race there has been a division between advocates of the persuit of strength and advocates of moderation.[22]

Our concern is not with the nature of these forces. Rather it is to apply our theoretical framework to the strategic arguments that prevailed in the formulation of nuclear policies. Did either or both sides aim at Sufficiency or Supremacy? Or did they pursue objectives in that middle ground where there is no logical basis for judging whether one strategy is better than another?

It is not easy to answer this question precisely. Policy is formulated in secret. Since it is the result of political compromises, it is not necessarily coherent. It is subject to great technological and institutional momentum. And it has many facets. Thus Des Ball, the leading researcher into the nuclear policies of the United States, distinguished five facets, 'not all of which are consistent with each other': *declaratory policy* 'which provides some official rationale for budgetary and other decisions, and the currency for most of the public debate about strategic policy, but. . .does not necessarily resemble at all closely how the United States would act in times of crisis or war'; *force development policy*, which concerns the size and characteristics of the forces that are acquired; *arms negotiation policy*, which concerns the balance to be sought and some guidance for the development of 'bargaining chips'; *operational policy*, which concerns such things as the deployment and alert rates of the nuclear forces that have been acquired; and *force employment policy* or *action policy*, which concerns how the United States would actually use its strategic forces in the event of a nuclear exchange.[23]

Incoherence and evasion are at their worst when it comes to nuclear decision-making in NATO, where all the member nations, nuclear and non-nuclear, whose opinions differ one from another, are invited to discuss and endorse the policies adopted by the United States for its nuclear forces in Europe, policies which the United States can scarcely be expected to put fully into commission since they determine the actions it should take with its nuclear weapons and the risks to which it exposes itself for the sake of its allies.[24] We know little about the decision-making process in the WTO.

In spite of these difficulties we can see some of the main outlines of nuclear policy. We have the benefit of vastly more evidence for the United States, which we shall consider first, than for the Soviet Union.

THE UNITED STATES

After 1945, and in the preceding years when the atomic bomb was being developed, the United States sought not to share nuclear weapons with the Soviet Union; and its reaction when the Soviet Union tested its first nuclear device in 1949 was to adopt NSC 68, a policy document suffused by a vivid fear of a Soviet global challenge, a fear provoked by Stalin's policy of gripping Eastern Europe, his challenges to the western Allies in Berlin and the outbreak of the Korean War.[25] This document, presented to President Truman in April 1950, put forward a policy 'to check and roll back the Kremlin's drive for world domination'[26] and 'simply took for granted. . . the imperative of a comprehensive effort to retain qualitative and quantitative nuclear superiority'.[27] Production of fissile material was greatly accelerated and it was decided to proceed with the development of the hydrogen bomb, referred to as the 'Super'. From 1948 to 1957, the commander of the US Strategic Air Command, was General Curtis LeMay, who believed in being able to win a decisive victory through a strategy of 'pre-emptive counterforce'. With the approval of the Joint Chiefs of Staff, he planned on that basis. In his words, 'I was prepared to beat him to the draw and attack all of his bomber and missile bases. In accordance with the Joint Chiefs of Staff my purpose was to destroy his war-making capability, particularly in the strategic nuclear area'.[28]

We can reasonably say of this period that the United States, when faced by the loss of its monopoly, sought Supremacy as best it could. But as the Soviet Union acquired nuclear weapons and managed swiftly to develop a hydrogen bomb, the notion that the United States could escape unacceptable damage receded in the minds of political leaders and the 'fading nuclear superiority' of the United States was acknowledged, even though a public stance and action policy appropriate to Supremacy was maintained.[29]

Since that period, nuclear policy has been in the no man's land between the pursuit of Sufficiency and the persuit of Supremacy. There has been 'a widespread aspiration that plans might be constructed which would allow the use of nuclear weapons in situations short of an all-out nuclear exchange.'[30] Superiority has repeatedly been sought in terms of numbers and war-fighting capability, even though it has been said repeatedly by political leaders that the Soviet Union and United States can destroy each other and cannot escape from that impasse.

Every kind of argument has been used to justify the acquisition of new and larger forces.

As United States arsenals increased it was argued that to deter the Soviet Union (i.e. for Sufficiency) you needed to be able to destroy not one, ten or 100 cities, but thousands of targets; and then that you needed to be able to threaten greater *relative* casualties and damage (with no absolute upper limit), so that the relative position of the Soviet Union and its prospects for recovery after a nuclear war would be worse than those of the United States.

There were false alarms that there was a bomber gap, that there was a missile gap, that the balance was 'delicate' and that there was a window of vulnerability, all meaning that the Soviet Union was getting ahead in a meaningful way.

It was argued that the United States must match or outclass the Soviet Union in weapons category by category (though categorisation is arbitrary), in order to avoid escalation dominance by the Soviet Union or pursue it for the United States.

It was argued in general terms that you must have flexibility because an 'all or nothing' stance is not credible as a basis for deterring anything other than the use of nuclear weapons by the other side, which is too passive a stance. Repeatedly a major ingredient in the compromises reached has been the idea that you must have a nuclear war-fighting capability, that you must be able to use and think about nuclear weapons in the same way as you use and think about non-nuclear weapons.

The main arguments for moderation have been made by reference to the need for stability, meaning the need to ensure that you and your opponent have a secure, invulnerable second strike forces so that there is no pressure for pre-emptive attack – an aim which is the opposite of the pursuit of Supremacy or any kind of superiority through the acquisition of war-fighting capabilities. But the pursuit of stability has fared badly compared with the pursuit of superiority. Perhaps the most significant episodes were the United States decision to introduce the most highly destabilising devices, MIRVs (multiple independently-targetable re-entry vehicles), during the negotiation of the SALT I Treaty (which stopped the introduction of anti-ballistic missile defences which MIRVs were designed to penetrate); and the decision immediately after the Treaty was concluded to proceed with the development and introduction of cruise missiles.[31]

All the arguments mentioned so far have some appearance of being strategic arguments even though they either lie in the no man's land where, for the reasons discussed in earlier chapters, there is no logic of strategy, only bluff; or they have rested upon strong assertions about the amount of destruction required to keep the Soviet Union at bay or the size of Soviet forces which were soon seen, or can now be seen, to have been ill-founded. For example, President Eisenhower in his memoirs described the bomber gap and the missile gap as 'nothing more than imaginative creations of irresponsibility'.[32]

There is another level of debate where two arguments have repeatedly been used which can readily be seen to have no foundation in strategy. They have nevertheless had a powerful persuasive effect in political debate. They are the arguments – or, rather, the assertions – that a proposed measure will 'strengthen deterrence' and that a proposed measure is necessary in order to 'preserve balance' in nuclear weapons. We shall examine them in turn.

STRENGTHENING DETERRENCE

To advocate a measure – usually a new weapons programme – on the grounds that it will strengthen deterrence is to imply that anything that strengthens deterrence is a good thing: it is to imply that deterrence is an end in itself, rather than a means to a political end.

As we have seen, what deter means, literally, is to keep someone at bay by threatening them – by fear. It follows that to say that it is a good thing to strengthen deterrence is to say that any step that increases the threat to your neighbour is a good thing; it makes the pursuit of such steps a proxy for a considered political aim. The question whether the political effects of a threatening military posture are desired is pre-judged or ignored. Those effects, as we have seen, are instability and negative feedback in the form of competitive arming and political tension. Those who argue that a measure is needed in order to strengthen deterrence usually do not say that these will be the effects nor ask whether they are desired.

But ambiguity makes the problem more complicated than this.

As discussion of nuclear strategy has spilled over into non-nuclear strategy, the word deterrence has come to be applied to any means of dissuading your neighbour from attacking you regardless of its nature. On this usage, you can *deter* your neighbour at the non-nuclear level either by a strategy of denial (through possession of defensive forces) or by a strategy of retaliation (through the possession of offensive forces).[33] The notion that the first is a defensive strategy, the second an offensive (retaliatory) strategy is lost. The words defence and deterrence are used interchangeably; and the word deterrence, as well as the word defence, is used with extreme ambiguity.

It is because the claim that a measure will strengthen deterrence confuses *both* political ends and means *and* the distinction between different military means, that it has had such great persuasive power.

It is a claim that sounds good; a politician propounding it can interpret it this way one minute and another the next, as he deals with criticism; and each person will himself read into it what satisfies his preconceptions. No less important, the ambiguity of 'deterrence' makes it inadvisable to use this word in rigorous discussion of strategy – unless definitions are first agreed upon explicitly, or implicitly through repeated usage in a group.

Because of the ambiguous way in which the words deter and deterrence have come to be used, I, as the reader may have noticed, have avoided them. My purpose, as I noted at the start, is to offer well-defined concepts in place of the ambiguities of deterrence, and, in particular, to distinguish political aims from military means.

THE PURSUIT OF BALANCE

I have dwelt in earlier chapters on the theoretical objections to the pursuit of balance in arms: it produces instability and negative feedback and, in the case of nuclear weapons, it implies that no heed should be paid to the fact that there is a saturation point.

What concerns me here is that it has been argued repeatedly that more nuclear weapons must be acquired if the other side is not to get ahead. To keep up, or ahead, in the pursuit of nuclear balance has been seen as a sign that the nation, or at least its leaders, possess political resolution, a sign that the status of the nation is being upheld. This can be seen most clearly in the United States and around NATO where this message has been conveyed, successfully, to the public by the military, the politicians and the commentators. The result is that it has been necessary for anyone seeking high office broadly to subscribe to the pursuit of balance. In the United States, the question whether the relative number of nuclear weapons has political significance when nuclear arsenals are past the saturation level, has been met by theorising about the psychological effects of nuclear superiority and nuclear inferiority under the title of 'perception theory'. It has been argued that because people perceive (albeit foolishly) that it matters whether you are superior or inferior in nuclear weapons, it matters; therefore you must make sure that you are not inferior or your opponent will get a psychological boost and hence a political advantage over you, who will be suffering a psychological sense of inadequacy. It is a proposition which, like the Emperor's clothes, rests on irrational belief alone. The comment has been made that, in nuclear strategy, perception theory is the last refuge of a scoundrel; but that has not prevented these notions from being politically effective in generating the pursuit of balance.[34]

In a recent enquiry, a sample of members of United States defence policy-makers, past and present, were questioned to see if they thought that new United States nuclear weapons which are capable of destroying hard targets were being built for objective strategic reasons or to serve psychological needs. A layered structure of rationales was found. In the first layer some ascribed a military need to the weapons but, when reminded of the problems with these arguments, 'abandoned them with surprising ease'. The second and most dominant layer of argument was that the weapons were needed to manipulate Soviet and European perceptions, but here there were problems 'which led respondents to make statements that seemed inconsistent and even confused'. Finally, at the deepest layer they used arguments based on concern for the 'psychological needs of the American people'.

Thus a government strategic analyst ended up saying, 'All roads in the strategic equation lead to MAD (mutual assured destruction). All the other ones are games, are window dressings, and they are window dressings for upmanship'. When asked, 'Why? To what end?', he replied, 'Prestige, self assurance'. And a State Department official said, 'if you want to discuss what buying weapons is about, it's to make yourself feel that you're doing your part for national defense. . . [Decision-makers] don't think through the use of weapons – nobody does. . . We don't only build to impress [the Soviets] – in part you build to impress yourself'. But he clarified that it is essential not to make it explicit that the weapons are being built for reasons other than security interests: 'You don't say to yourself, "We're building this so. . . we'll feel better"'.[35]

THE SOVIET UNION

The fact that the Soviet Union came to possess a nuclear arsenal of the same size as the United States, and of similar composition, if allowance is made for differences in geography, indicates that the nuclear policies of the two competing nations were – or came to be – much the same as regards the most significant facet of nuclear policy – nuclear force development, which determines nuclear capabilities.

We can infer that the Soviet Union did not rest content with Sufficiency. Admittedly, it is hard to tell whether the very limited Soviet arsenal of strategic nuclear weapons in the early 1960s was the result of calculated restraint or unavoidable economic-cum-technological constraints. One story with some plausibility would be that the Soviet Union thought intercontinental missiles so potent a novelty that they did not initially plan for many; only after they saw the huge United States programmes for long-range missiles and suffered the humiliation of having to withdraw medium-range missiles from Cuba did they go for big programmes and a policy of catching up. The alternative explanation is that they never accepted the notion of inferiority and, having deployed many medium-range nuclear missiles in Europe, were held back in the deployment of long-range missiles only by technical-cum-economic constraints. Some mixture of the two explanations is possible. What is clear is that the Soviet Union caught up in the late 1960s or early 1970s.

At the other extreme, it does not seem plausible that the Soviet Union, having been second to acquire nuclear weapons and preoccupied with catching up, quantitatively and qualitatively, ever thought it could achieve nuclear Supremacy in the sense in which we have it, though, as we shall see, the idea of achieving relative strength was part of its declaratory policy.

This being so, we can say that the Soviet Union's policies, like those of the United States, lay in the no man's land where catching up, achieving balance or superiority and avoiding inferiority, were dominant considerations; and we can be sure that, as in any other country, the decisions were compromises reached in a political process and will not always have been rational and coherent.

The literature on Soviet nuclear doctrine tells us little about the arguments actually used in the determination of policy, but some stand out that are relevant to our enquiry.

First, although there seems to be no evidence that Soviet strategic theorists appealed to perception theory or advocated relative strength for the sake of its psychological effects, the importance attached to catching up and to the achievement of parity with the United States, whatever the reasons for it, had the effect of lending symbolic importance to relative numbers of nuclear weapons.

Secondly, in expositions of the new doctrine established under Mr Gorbachev, it is emphasised that previous Soviet doctrine, which was in force from the beginning of the nuclear era, laid down that it was the task of *foreign policy to prevent war*; the task of the *armed forces to win a war*, should it occur; for this purpose, the armed forces must be prepared to conduct resolute offensive operations at all levels.[36] Nuclear weapons were assimilated into this approach and treated as another weapon which was bound to be used in the event of war. They were not treated as a special category requiring a special theoretical approach. There was here a doctrinal basis for the justification of war-fighting strategies.

Thirdly, in the 1950s and 1960s it was argued that the Soviet Union would win a nuclear war because the peoples would be the victors through revolutionary zeal, and from this faith it followed that the task for the military was to do their best to ensure victory.

None of these three points seems to have been radically challenged, though some of them were moderated and modified, until Mr Gorbachev introduced his new thinking, a subject we shall look at later.

THE LESSER NUCLEAR POWERS

There are two categories of lesser nuclear powers, those that declare that they possess nuclear weapons and those that deny it (or claim that they have developed nuclear devices only for peaceful purposes).

In the first category are Britain, China and France, all of which have nuclear arsenals that satisfy or exceed our notions of Sufficiency but are much smaller than the arsenals of the Soviet Union and United States. Since they could not catch up with the Soviet Union and United States, these three powers have had to appeal, implicitly or explicitly, to a doctrine of Sufficiency. Whether they like it or not, they have been unable to pursue balance; they have not been able to appeal to any of the arguments for balance or superiority and have lived perfectly well without them. For the rest they face just the same inescapable dilemmas of nuclear doctrine as the Soviet Union and United States. In their declared policies, emphasis varies between the notion that nuclear weapons serve to prevent 'nuclear blackmail', i.e. to prevent the threat of use of nuclear weapons, and the notion that they serve to prevent non-nuclear attacks; and between the position taken by Britain, that its nuclear weapons exist to deter a specified nuclear power (the Soviet Union), the position taken at one time by France that its nuclear weapons are not pointed at anyone in particular and the position taken by China that it will never be the first to use its nuclear weapons which serve to keep the two 'superpowers' at bay.

The nations which deny that they possess nuclear weapons but appear to possess them, which are India, Israel and South Africa, are interesting in that they appear to regard the veiled threat, the quiet reminder, as preferable in their circumstances to a more explicit and challenging posture *vis-à-vis* their potential opponents. One can see various possible reasons for adoption of this posture. Openly to declare possession of nuclear weapons and to state in what circumstances you might use them might be more likely to cause your potential enemies to hasten to acquire nuclear weapons for themselves than a quiet posture which surrounds your possession of them with some uncertainty. To conceal and deny what you are doing while you are developing nuclear weapons may help to prevent existing nuclear powers from being as vigilant as they might otherwise be in withholding items that you need or in applying other sanctions to you. And, if you have denied that you seek nuclear weapons while you are developing them, it may be awkward openly to declare later that you have been practising deception and now possess them.

But these arguments are not so powerful that they would prevail if there were felt to be a substantial military advantage in making explicit rather than implicit the threat that you might use nuclear weapons. That these nations have gone for the implicit threat while others, principally the Soviet Union and the United States, have gone for the explicit threat is an illustration of the point that there is no means of knowing whether a quiet threat or a noisy threat will be more effective (Chapter 3).

DISARMAMENT AND ARMS CONTROL

New life has been breathed into arms negotiations – and into strategy – since Mr Gorbachev came to power. But before discussing these recent happenings, it is useful to look at the previous pattern of arms negotiations.

The main feature of arms negotiations after 1945 was the displacement of disarmament by arms control. Disarmament, meaning the cessation of competition in arms and the elimination of arms through negotiations, had been pursued without success before 1914 and between the wars (see Appendix). In 1945, the desire to eliminate arms and settle disputes peacefully was alive again and, with the creation of the UN, disarmament was again on the international agenda. But as the Cold War was joined and security was sought through the strategy of arming and mutual threats, disarmament was laid aside. Proposals for general disarmament were presented to the public by each side, but the proposals were commonly so constructed that they were not acceptable to the other side.[37] Nothing came of them. Disarmament negotiations in which countries from all parts of the world take part have continued, but they have been narrowed down to the discussion in slow motion of small limited measures.

Arms control, which began to displace disarmament in the 1950s and then came to dominate arms negotiations between the Soviet Union and the United States, was invented in the United States as an adjunct of nuclear deterrence. The rationale for it has been that, if two powers armed with nuclear weapons confront each other in a nuclear setting and are restrained from attacking each other only by the threat of mutual destruction, they nevertheless have some common interests with respect to their military conduct that are worth discussing and trying to agree upon.

The advent of arms control has been described as 'a shift in emphasis towards the notion of managing rather than eliminating the arms race'.[38] In practice, the term 'arms control', which is ambiguous, has commonly been extended to cover all types of arms negotiation. But the core of it has the idea that nuclear adversaries might pursue common interests while directly threatening each other.

Three main areas can be identified in which the pursuit of common interests has been attempted. The first has been the negotiation of confidence-building measures, meaning for example measures to improve communication between the two sides and set rules for encounters between the military of the two sides at frontiers or at sea with the object of preventing accidental war and allaying alarmist fears. In this area there is a simple convergence of interests. Nobody wants accidents. The two sides have been rather successful in reaching agreements.

The second area is nuclear non-proliferation, which means preventing others getting nuclear weapons. This can be regarded as primarily a policy which contributes to the safety of the world or primarily a policy which helps maintain the monopoly of nuclear power for those who have nuclear weapons. Either way it is evident that on this issue the interests of the top nuclear powers converge – though their attitude may not quickly be shared by those who manage to defy them and develop nuclear weapons on their own. As you would predict, they have united in the pursuit of non-proliferation. (Whether they have achieved much in substance is another matter.)

The third area is negotiation over the level and character of forces. Here it is evident that there has not been a convergence of interests between the two sides and that there could not be such a convergence given the strategies they have followed. For those strategies have meant that the two sides have engaged in negotiation over forces that have high offensive capability; the pursuit of relative strength has therefore been a prime objective; and for that purpose each side has tried to limit tightly those catagories of weapon where the other side has an advantage in terms of the weapons it actually possesses or is likely to develop in the period ahead, while at the same time seeking to keep as free a hand as possible in those categories of weapon where it enjoys an actual or potential advantage. A further justification sometimes offered for this tactic has been the bargaining chip argument – that if you pursue and achieve superiority you will bring the other side to the bargaining table – an argument which can be seen to be flawed as soon as you consider the possibility that both sides might use it. When an agreement has been made, it has commonly been circumvented by the development of new weapons just beyond the fringes of the agreement. In sum, arms control negotiations have been, as they were intended to be, an adjunct of the arms race – at any rate until recently.

That the arms race was not impeded greatly, if at all, is evident from the rate at which arms have been accumulated since the 1950s. Incidentally, there has been an output of a different kind. Several decades of negotiation have brought into being large negotiating teams, manned by members of the diplomatic services, the armed forces and other parts of the bureaucracies of the negotiating nations. These armies of people accustomed to adversarial negotiation have lived for years in Geneva and the other cities where they meet. They are backed at home by teams of similar people who formulate policy and draw up the instructions for the negotiators. And there has grown up around them an army of journalists, commentators and politicians who have acquired knowledge of weapons and negotiating positions. Adversarial negotiation has been a booming industry.

At the multilateral negotiations, mostly held in Geneva, a few agreements have been reached which outlaw activities peripheral to the main arms race, for example, the agreements not to use the Antarctic for military purposes, not to test nuclear weapons above ground and not to fix nuclear weapons to the sea bed. An important treaty was made prohibiting the production and possession of bacteriological weapons and toxins – a genuine disarmament measure with respect to a category of weapons which, if developed and used, would be highly dangerous and uncontrollable. And then there have been the treaties to limit nuclear proliferation – the Non-proliferation Treaty and the Latin American and South Pacific nuclear-free zones – but these treaties have not been subscribed to by nations with nuclear ambitions.

In the strategic nuclear field, three treaties were made between the Soviet Union and United States before the recent thaw began. SALT I (1972) limited the number of strategic missiles and strategic bombers, but, as was noted earlier, it was undermined while it was still being negotiated by the decision to introduce more warheads into each missile in the form of MIRVs and, after it was concluded, by the development of cruise missiles, which were not covered by the treaty. The ABM treaty (1972) narrowly limited the deployment of anti-ballistic missile defences, but it has been threatened by the American SDI programme to develop defences and its Soviet counterpart. SALT II (signed in 1979) set limits to strategic warhead numbers as well as delivery vehicles. It was rejected by the US Senate in 1980 but it does not seem to have been greatly breached.

At the non-nuclear level, the Mutual Balanced Force Reduction talks (MBFR talks) over the number of persons in the forces of the two alliances in Europe have been a charade. At nearly 500 meetings the opposed negotiating teams have argued inconclusively for 15 years about what numbers of conventional troops on each side would represent a balance. It has been suggested that this outcome has represented a success for NATO, on the grounds that it engaged in these multilateral talks only in order to prevent unilateral withdrawals of United States troops from Europe.[39]

No agreements were reached with respect to other non-nuclear weapons or forces, apart from the bacteriological weapons treaty, noted earlier, and the agreements on Confidence-Building Measures, which in recent years have provided, most usefully, for such things as the issuing of advance warnings of manoeuvres and the sending of inspectors to them.

That arms control treaties should have done little to retard the arms race is understandable. If, as has predominantly been the case in the confrontation between the two alliances, the basis of strategy has been the making of threats and the pursuit of balance or, better still, relative strength for that purpose, it is only to be expected that arms negotiations, which are a means of implementing a strategy, will be directed to the pursuit of those aims. Admittedly, the concept of arms control was suffused with persuasive ambiguity. In response to the feeling amongst politicians and the public that something needed to be done to check the nuclear arms race, the notion that arms control would produce disarmament was sometimes given considerable emphasis in public. But when it came to determining policy and getting the support of the military and the other political power brokers, it is pretty clear that in the United States the pursuit of relative strength generally came out on top, as it was almost bound to do so long as strategy was based on making the threat to the other side as powerful as possible. And, though there is little evidence to go by, it is clear from Soviet actions that they sought relative strength and were not ready in the pre-Gorbachev era to sacrifice relative strength for the sake of agreements to limit or reduce arms. In short, it sometimes appeared – notably in popular political statements – that disarmament and the ending of confrontation were the aim of arms control, but the aim that prevailed, dictated by the accepted strategies of the two sides, was to maintain or maximise the threat to the other side.

In arms negotiations, as in other areas of strategy, the choices of political aims and of alternative ways of pursuing those aims were lost to sight. The maintenance of the maximum threat of nuclear retaliation was accepted as the aim of strategy in a nuclear setting with scant regard to other ways of seeking security or of the feedback that this strategy generated; and from that undersized notion of strategy was derived the idea of arms control as a means of managing the risks, or at least avoiding unintended risks.

Developments in arms negotiations since Mr Gorbachev came to power are considered in Chapter 7.

7 The Present Position and the Policy Alternatives

Over the past few years relations between East and West have improved to the point where there has appeared to be a possibility that the confrontation between NATO and the WTO might be ended if military strategy, including arms negotiations, together with other aspects of international relations, were directed to that purpose on both sides. The biggest and most dramatic change has been in the policies of the Soviet Union since Mr Gorbachev came to power in 1985. There had been some improvement before then, but there were setbacks. The tide of change moved hesitantly until Mr Gorbachev introduced his 'new thinking' about the whole Soviet system and announced radical new policies deriving from it. He has declared the conflict which lay behind the Cold War to be over, and in his policies of openness, increasing respect for human rights, democratisation, economic reform with emphasis on the market and his foreign policy of withdrawing from military intervention and seeking cooperative solutions to international problems, he has taken a set of steps towards the fulfilment of his declared aims.

SOVIET AND WTO POLICY

To meet the major change in the Soviet political aims, Soviet military doctrine has been through a major review. In this review an important part appears to have been played by civilian defence analysts, a new breed of experts whose intellectual formation was in the research institutes which study the West. They are well versed in all the arguments, old and new, in circulation in the West, including the arguments for defensive defence.

The main changes in doctrine appear to be these:

1. The aim of military doctrine is no longer to *win* a war should it occur, with the prevention of war left to foreign policy. The new aim of military doctrine at all levels is to *prevent* war.[1]
2. The Soviet objective for their forces under the new doctrine is 'Reasonable Sufficiency' which has been interpreted by Mr

111

Gorbachev as follows: 'The path towards the realisation of Reasonable Sufficiency we see in governments not having more military strength and armaments than is necessary for their reliable defence, and also in their armed forces being structured in such a way that they will provide all that is needed for the repulsion of any possible aggression but could not be used for offensive purposes.'[2] It has been stated that an important reason for the change in doctrine was that in the course of the review of Soviet military doctrine it was recognised that the old offensive doctrine caused negative feedback, politically and in arming.[3]

3. The WTO in May 1987 issued an agreed statement on doctrine which seemed to combine the new defensive doctrine with bits left over from the old offensive doctrine. The statement repeated the old retaliatory slogan that in the event of war the Warsaw Pact forces would deliver a devastating rebuff to the aggressor; it called for the establishment between NATO and the WTO of a balance of forces at a lower level, for consultations between the two alliances on the removal of imbalances in separate types of armaments and services of the armed forces, for consultations with the aim of comparing doctrines and ensuring that the doctrines and concepts of the two alliances are based on defensive principles, and it called for the eventual simultaneous dissolution of the two pacts.[4]

4. The Soviet Union has called for deep cuts in nuclear weapons and for their eventual elimination.

5. The Soviet Union, having previously resisted on-site inspection for the purpose of verifying arms agreements and thereby put a major obstacle in the way of arms agreements, has become an advocate and practitioner of open verification.

These changes in policy could be interpreted as the adoption by the WTO of the military objectives of nuclear Sufficiency and non-nuclear Defensive Superiority, the objectives appropriate to peaceful aims. But some of the old doctrine lurks in the references to delivering a devastating rebuff (without the qualification that these words refer to nuclear weapons only) and in the insistence on balance. From this evidence and from the open discussion of these matters one now meets in the Soviet Union, it is pretty clear that, as you would expect, there is an Old Guard in the military, and probably in other groups within the Soviet Union, who do not welcome the radical change in doctrine that is being introduced.[5]

There is also reason to believe that the smaller members of the WTO hold differing positions.

As regards negotiations over non-nuclear forces, the WTO proposed that the Vienna talks should proceed in three stages:

1. Remove imbalances and asymmetries in forces, concentrating on the most destabilising types, so as to produce a balance rather lower than the level of forces on the higher side.
2. Cut the general levels of forces, including personnel, from the level reached in stage 1.
3. Restructure the remaining forces to make them defensive.

These proposals were followed by President Gorbachev's announcement at the United Nations in December 1988 of substantial unilateral cuts and a reduction of Soviet forces in Eastern Europe. The proposal that restructuring should come only at stage 3 seems at odds with the insistence by the Soviet authorities that they have started implementing their new defensive doctrine and are beginning to restructure some of their divisions.

NATO POLICIES

On its side, NATO has not produced a new doctrine. Rather it has continued to defend its doctrine of Flexible Response and to implement its new policies of FOFA, which are threatening in the eyes of the WTO. But in response to the WTO initiatives on arms negotiation, NATO has made proposals which show flexibility.

In December 1986 NATO agreed in Brussels a declaration on arms control which reiterated its commitment to 'an effective and credible deterrent posture' and emphasised the need for a balance of forces. With respect to future negotiations over conventional forces, the statement proposed a 'focus on the elimination of the capacity for surprise attack' and 'further measures to build confidence and to improve openness and calculability about military behaviour'.[6] In December 1988, after the WTO had announced its change in doctrine and its three stage approach to the Vienna negotiations on conventional forces, NATO agreed a new statement which called as a first step for the removal of imbalances by reductions in key offensive armaments (e.g. tanks) to rather below the level of the lower side (usually NATO), for greater 'transparency' through steps in the nature of confidence-building measures and for talks on doctrine. It concluded by calling for the implementation of these proposals and saying that 'in the light of their implementation, we would then be willing to contemplate' further reductions and 'the restructuring of armed forces to enhance defensive capabilities and further reduce offensive capabilities'.[7]

ARMS NEGOTIATIONS

In negotiation, the main achievement has been the INF Agreement which rids Europe of all intermediate-range, land-based nuclear ballistic missiles and cruise missiles. This agreement was reached when the Soviet Union accepted the most radical proposal previously offered by the United States, plus full verification, and the United States, with the agreement of its allies, stood by its old offer. This concrete demonstration of sincerity by both sides, followed by the scrapping of forbidden missiles in the presence of observers from both sides probably did more to change the atmosphere than all the talk that went before.

At the Strategic Arms Reduction Talks (START) where the Soviet Union and United States have the objective of making cuts of approximately 50 per cent in strategic nuclear weapons, the main doctrinal issue concerns defences. As we have seen, defences against nuclear weapons are destabilising and more consistent with the pursuit of Supremacy than the pursuit of Sufficiency. The United States, having adopted the vast but now reduced SDI programme to develop defences, is reluctant to abandon the programme, while the Soviet's declared position is to stop the development of defences.

At the non-nuclear level, the positions taken by the two sides mean that there is the following common ground:

- There is recognition of the need to reduce the possibility of surprise attack (which means any attack, since if a surprise attack is impossible, so is an unsurprising attack).
- It is recognised that it is possible to identify weapons and forces which are necessary for attack and that reductions in these weapons will reduce the possibilities of attack, i.e. will increase stability.
- It is recognised that restructuring to increase defensive capabilities relative to offensive capabilities is possible and should be tackled at some stage.

–   But the first step proposed by both sides is the achievement of a *balance* in the selected offensive armaments at a level little lower than that of the weaker side.

There is a contradiction here. On the one hand, the commitment to reduce the risk of surprise attack and to move on to restructuring implies that the common objective is to reduce offensive armaments to a level which is low in relation to defensive capabilities – in other words to pursue Mutual Defensive Superiority. That, as we have seen, is the right way to end a confrontation and stop an arms race at the non-nuclear level. On the other hand, both sides proposed that the first step to be pursued is a balance in each of the selected offensive items, which is not a condition of stability: as we have seen, to equalise the strength of mobile armoured forces at a level that is not clearly below the defensive capabilities of the two sides is to create a situation where each side may fear attack by the other (Chapter 4).

In mitigation of this contradiction in the common approach, it can be said that the agreement to reduce major offensive armaments to a common level so as to remove 'asymmetries' is a major concession by the WTO military, who have previously pursued, and apparently possessed, superiority in the key types of non-nuclear armament needed for an offensive; and it must seem a reassuring first step to the NATO military who have previously felt numerically inferior. Moreoever the risks of surprise attack, and the pressures for pre-emption which go with equal offensive forces, may be mitigated by confidence-building measures. On these grounds it may be argued that it is a reasonable first step.

But an important way to judge a first step is by whether it is well calculated to produce further steps. On this score there are grounds for concern.

In the first place, because balance cannot be defined precisely, to attempt to negotiate a balance in forces that have a high offensive capability is, as we have seen, a classic recipe for an impasse caused by disputes over definitions and numbers (Chapter 5).

Secondly, either side may still be tempted to take independent actions to improve its offensive strength while negotiations are taking place. The problem has arisen over short-range nuclear weapons in Europe, a category of weapon which is outside present negotiating mandates and for which NATO has a major modernisation programme. For the moment NATO has postponed the decision to deploy the weapons. But the problem of preventing perverse independent actions which impede the negotiation of arms limitation treaties, or undermine their efficacy after they come into effect, is not confined to this category of weapon. To prevent the acquisition of destabilising offensive forces requires the general modification of existing military programmes in a defensive direction. And that requires the implementation of new strategies by both sides.[8] If, at the non-nuclear level, a strategy of denial and the stance of Mutual Defensive Superiority had been adopted and were being implemented by both sides, each would have stopped enhancing its offensive capability while seeking to limit that of the other side; each would be concerned instead with the task of removing offensive forces from both sides and restructuring the remaining forces so as to maximise their defensive capability. At the nuclear level, if each side had adopted the stance of Sufficiency and was seeking to reduce nuclear arsenals, the development of new defences against each other's strategic nuclear weapons would have been abandoned.

The fact is that the strategies of the two sides are in flux, with each side reacting to what the other does by way of independent actions, consultation and negotiation. As we have seen, the WTO, led by the Soviet Union, has changed its declared non-nuclear doctrine to defensiveness but, in proposing the negotiation of a balance of forces as the first step in that direction, it has been rather less than whole-hearted in the implementation of that doctrine. NATO has so far stuck to its old doctrine, but it has agreed on a negotiating programme for non-nuclear forces which, if it is carried out successfully, will render that doctrine obsolete: the doctrine of Flexible Response and NATO's commitment to the First Use of nuclear weapons were adopted because there was an imbalance in non-nuclear forces in favour of the WTO and a real fear of a non-nuclear surprise attack by the WTO, two conditions which the first stage of the negotiations on non-nuclear forces is designed to remove. Authoritative people around NATO, for example the director of the International Institute for Strategic Studies, have begun to recognise that NATO needs to prepare itself for a change in doctrine.[9]

The adoption and implementation of new strategic doctrines is not a narrow technical matter which can be left to the military and those concerned with arms negotiations. It requires a political choice at the highest level, followed up by clear political direction of the military and of those who direct and conduct negotiation; and it needs to be combined with cooperative and reassuring policies between the two alliances in non-military matters.[10]

An argument that is sometimes made against a change in NATO strategy is that it would mean 'lowering your guard'; and that to do that would be unwise, since President Gorbachev may run into such great domestic difficulties that the present favourable tide of Soviet policy is checked or reversed. Certainly the Soviet Union has such a distorted economic and social system that, having begun to release that system, it probably faces many years of political tension; and the chances, which cannot be known, that those conditions will cause the Soviet Union to revert to a more hostile attitude to the rest of the world cannot be dismissed as zero. It is therefore only prudent to ask if a change in strategy by NATO would mean that it lowered its guard. The answer is that a change of strategy of the kind we propose means the opposite. To go for non-nuclear Mutual Defensive Superiority (with the WTO making much the larger cuts) is to keep up your guard while reducing the punch it has to meet. The more rational way to overcome fear of a future change in policy in the Soviet Union would be to try to change the strategy and force structures of both sides as fast as possible. A reversal of Soviet policy while present force levels and force structures were still in being would be more dangerous from a military point of view than a reversal after the change had been made.

Another cause of hesitation in NATO appears to be a fear that if the East–West military confrontation is ended, the alliances will break up and there will be the risk of conflict in Europe as old quarrels between neighbours, no longer contained by the alliance structure, break out again, or as Germany reunites and again becomes a strong power in an unstable position in the centre of Europe. Whatever the validity of these fears, it is far from clear that attempts to resist a change in strategic doctrine will hold NATO together rather than split it: the alliance might best achieve harmony and be able to move together if it changed strategy. Beyond, there is the question what new security regime might later be established for Europe. There is no great difficulty in setting out military designs for alternative new regimes, if the political structure is specified. What that should be is another subject.

Appendix: Disarmament Negotiations before 1945

Attempts to negotiate international reductions in arms began nearly one hundred years ago and in some respects have followed a rather repetitive pattern. The pattern of negotiations since 1945 has been discussed in Chapters 6 and 7. Before that, there were two phases of negotiation – the negotiations at the Hague conferences before 1914, and the inter-war disarmament negotiations centred in Geneva. This Appendix sketches the background to those two phases of negotiations and then looks at how arms negotiations were approached in order to see what lessons can be learnt that may be useful today. The two periods are considered in turn.

A NEGOTIATIONS BEFORE 1914

The Background

To read the history of the period before 1914 today is to be reminded how unstable, compared to today, were the relationships between the countries of Europe in that period. While there was no war beween the major powers from 1871 to 1914, this was not because the major powers refrained from competing with one another for power, prestige, territory or empire. Far from it, they competed with one another with a chauvinism which, seen from Europe today, looks startlingly brash – though it may not look like that when viewed from the perspective of today's 'superpowers'.

Continental frontiers had all recently been changed by war. German unity had been forged by three wars: Prussia (with Austria) had invaded Schleswig Holstein in 1864; she had defeated Austria and expanded southward in 1866; and had defeated France and taken Alsace Lorraine in 1871. The six Great Powers – in alphabetical order, Austria–Hungary, Britain, France, Germany, Italy and Russia – that emerged in this age of nationalism and unification had struggled with one another in the decades preceding 1914 over their own frontiers, over the Balkans and the relics of the Ottoman empire, and over imperial territories in other continents. From day to day the politico–economic competition took the form of the making of alliances or informal understandings, in which you made promises about the conditions which you would or would not go to war in support of the country you were talking to, or its potential enemy. The promises could not be relied upon. If self-interest dictated that a country should or should not go to war, it could not be relied upon act in a contrary manner in fulfilment of a promise.

The immediate responsibility for the outbreak of war in 1914 is generally attributed to Germany, but there is a vast, inevitably inconclusive, literature on the underlying causes of the First World War.[1] At one extreme there are explanations in terms of objective economic factors. Thus it can be argued that the fundamental trouble was the breakdown in the balance of power as it had operated earlier in the nineteenth century. Germany which, through unification, industrialisation and militarisation, had swept ahead in power, occupied a position in the centre of Europe where her neighbours, feeling threatened by her, faced an inducement to combine against her to protect themselves. Britain was losing her industrial leadership, and she was preoccupied with empire.[2] At the other extreme there are explanations in terms to personalities: Germany was prudent so long as Bismarck was at the helm but became increasingly imprudent after Kaiser Wilhelm II had taken the helm.

In contrast to today, in the years before 1914 there was general acceptance of war as a means of settling differences. As August 1914 approached there was a feeling that war must come sooner or later, that it was a matter of seizing the initiative or waiting to respond, propelled or constrained by the behaviour of your neighbours, by domestic political pressures and by domestic opinion as it became more or less bellicose. The tides of opinion were not of course spontaneous. Monarchs, politicians and military leaders led opinion, sometimes with powerful effect; but once a mood had been generated, those who inspired it could not necessarily control it – or ignore it.

An important element in the situations was militarism, meaning not just the acceptance and glorification of war but the influence of the military on the course of military events.

The American president's personal envoy to Europe on a peace-making mission before the war reported that, 'The situation is extraordinary. It is militarism run stark mad. Unless someone acting for you can bring about a different understanding there is some day to be an awful cataclysm. There is too much hatred, too many jealousies'.[3]

The years before 1914, says an English historian, 'provide a terrible indictment of the self-defeating quest for national security through secret diplomacy and armed might. Psychologically, too, nations were being conditioned for war: by propaganda; by the spurious application of the Darwinian struggle to the human species; by bitter class divisions; and not least by self-delusion as to the nature of war.'[4]

The military were politically extraordinarily powerful in Germany:

> While the general acceptance of military values by large sections of the German public may have contributed to the mood which made war possible and to the enthusiasm with which the outbreak of war was greeted, the most important aspect of the role of the German army in the coming of war was its freedom from civilian political control. The Kaiser was the 'supreme war lord' and the army leaders were responsible to him alone. He had a personal military staff which operated independently of his civil and naval staffs, and the Chief of the General Staff had direct access to him. It was thus possible for military decisions to be taken without the knowledge of the civilian branches of the government – or indeed of the naval authorities. There was no collective leadership or responsibility. The only co-ordinating power lay with the Kaiser himself; and Wilhelm II was a wayward, capricious and unstable monarch incapable of pursuing a consistent course or controlling his advisers.[5]

A further element in the situation was that at this time offensive doctrine pervaded military thinking.

There appear to have been three main reasons why this was so. First there was a problem of 'the strong country in the middle (Chapter 2). Germany could only be kept at bay by her neighbours, France and Russia, if they both kept offensive forces so that each could attack or threaten to attack Germany if she attacked or threatened to attack the other.

Secondly, there was at this time a cult of the offensive amongst the military. This found its most extreme expression in France but it was by no means confined to France.[6] Much has been written about it recently.[7] What is most remarkable is that the idea of pressing home attacks with the bayonet was glorified at the time when the machine gun, which made bayonet attacks suicidal, had been developed and proven in a number of wars – admittedly wars conducted far away (the American Civil War, the Russo–Japanese War and fighting in Africa, including the Battle of Omdurman). There had been reports by military observers of the American Civil War that the improvement in fire power consequent on the introduction of breech-loading magazine rifles helped the defense and was rendering obsolete the massed attack.

Foch's prize pupil, Grandmaison, proclaimed the doctrine of the offensive in the official regulations of the French Army in the following terms:

> The French Army, returning to its traditions, no longer knows any other law than the offensive. . . All attacks are to be pushed to the extreme. . . to charge the enemy with the bayonet in order to destroy him. . . This result can only be obtained at the price of bloody sacrifice. Any other conception ought to be rejected as contrary to the very nature of war.[8]

As Liddell Hart commented,

> The theory of mass suffered a rude shock. Calculated to achieve success by a process of concentrating superior numbers at a so-called decisive spot, the formula was nullified by the mechanical progress which made one man sitting behind a machine the superior of a hundred, sometimes a thousand, who were advancing upon him with a bayonet. The more ranks of attackers, the more swathes of dead – that was all. The problem could only be solved by recourse to art – by developing new weapons, by creating surprise, or by taking advantage of obscurity, whether darkness or fog.[9]

Liddell Hart interpreted the cult of the offensive as an example of how slow the military are to adapt to technical change and learn the lessons of wars in which they have not been engaged. But that explanation implies that the military are indiscriminate in their opposition to technical progress. As Lawrence Freedman has observed,

> The military tend to have an ambivalent attitude to technological advance. They will embrace readily those incremental developments that allow them to perform their traditional roles even

better, but view with suspicion anything new that appears to require departures from established methods or, worse still, suggests the progressive obsolescence of their own brand of warfare.[10]

In this vein it has been argued that before 1914 the machine gun was despised and given too low priority by army officers in Britain and other countries because it represented the industrialisation of war: its adoption would mean that gentlemen devoted to horses and chivalry would be replaced by their social inferiors who understood machinery.[11]

Thirdly, it was believed and said on all sides that if there was a war it would be short, a proposition which required, and no doubt helped to promote, belief in the offensive. For if the defensive was superior, no quick conclusion would be reached. I. S. Bloch, a Warsaw banker who gave up banking to study the political economy of war and was a member of the Russian Council of State,[12] had predicted correctly that the increase in accurate firepower meant that the defence was coming into the ascendant. In a six-volume work in Russian, which was published in abridged form in English in 1899, he argued that there would be a stalemate, a ghastly war of attrition on an extended front, accompanied by economic strangulation.[13] His views were taken up in the peace movement, and reportedly may have contributed to the Tsar's decision to propose the Hague Conference, but otherwise they were not sympathetically received by political or military leaders.[14] To voice Bloch's predictions would not have helped sustain the fighting spirit of the armed forces and the people.

Finally, the arms race may have accentuated the emphasis on the offensive. The competitive development of new weapons and larger armed forces gathered momentum around the turn of the century as the Industrial Revolution spread and advanced, providing nations with a technical base and rising incomes, both of which could be harnessed for military purposes. Military expenditure as a share of national income was driven competitively upwards in the years before 1914. While the competition in arms was an expression of political rivalry, it added to the sense that relative strength must be pursued and must be exploited when you had achieved it. The most intense and extravagant aspect of the arms race was the competition in battleships between Britain and Germany.

The Naval Arms Race

The naval arms race before 1914 is fascinatingly like the nuclear arms race between the two 'Super Powers' since 1945. In the nuclear arms race, the United States started with a monopoly of nuclear weapons. Once the Soviet Union had learned how to make nuclear weapons and began to develop its own force, the race was on. In the earlier case, Britain started with an extraordinary mastery of the sea; it had a fleet far larger than any other single nation; it regarded mastery of the seas as necessary to the maintenance of the formal and informal empire on which its wealth, trade and national ego depended. Until the early 1900s, 'the construction of the German navy had been regarded as a harmless hobby of the Kaiser's'.[15] After the turn of the century, when Germany began to build on a larger scale and relations between Britain and Germany were damaged by German expressions of sympathy for the Boers, the expansion of the German fleet began to cause concern. The first Lord of the Admiralty, Lord Selborne, warned the Cabinet that 'The naval policy of Germany is definite and persistent. The Emperor seems determined that the power of Germany shall be used all over the world to push German commerce, possessions and interests.'[16] And in October 1902 he went a step further warning that, 'The more the composition of the new German fleet is examined the clearer it becomes that it is designed for a possible conflict with the British fleet.'[17]

The British response to the German challenge lay in naval reform and modernisation. Expenditure on the navy had already more than doubled between 1889 and 1900; it increased by 30 per cent between 1900 and 1904.[18] The driving force behind the transformation of the navy from a traditional service with slow ships of uncertain reliability to a modern service with ships of high reliability that stretched technology to its limits, was Admiral Fisher, whose belligerence and colourful behaviour remind one of some of the American champions of the nuclear arms race, for example, Admiral Rickover who pushed through the introduction of Polaris submarines firing missiles from under water, or General Curtis LeMay. It is worth quoting at some length how Marder, in his excellent naval history of this period, describes Fisher:

Much has been made of the ferocity with which he always spoke on the subject of war. 'War should be terrible', he said, and there is his oft-quoted statement at the Hague Peace Conference of 1899: 'The humanizing of war! You might as well talk of humanizing Hell. . . as if war could be civilized.' In reality, there was nothing blood-thirsty about Fisher. He was a man of peace and it was his conviction that war was the greatest idiocy of life. But once it happened, he urged, it must not be conducted weakly. 'My sole object is PEACE. . . if you "rub it in" both at home and abroad that you are ready for instant war with every unit of your strength in the first line, and intend to be "first in" and hit your enemy in the belly and kick him when he's down and boil your prisoners in oil (*if you take any!*) and torture his women and children, then people will keep clear of you.' In other words, as he often expressed the same thought, it was the duty of the British Fleet to 'hit first, to hit hard, and keep on hitting', so that by one collossal effort the enemy might be destroyed and the nation saved from all the horrors of a long-drawn-out series of indecisive contests.

Fisher's jingoism is supposed to be proved by his 'plans' for a preventive war. In private conversations with intimate friends he did put forward the idea. . . It was never considered by the Board and it was never part of British naval policy in the Fisher administration.

Regrettably, as so often happens in history, the legend was far more important than the fact. Many Germans in responsible positions, the Emperor among them, really believed that Fisher planned to attack, a feeling reinforced by occasional preventive war speeches and articles in England. This will explain at least some of the German jitteriness in 1904–5.[19]

Tirpitz was, like Fisher, a brilliant organizer and a great leader, indefatigable, resourceful, and utterly unscrupulous in methods.[20]

During the debates over naval building programmes and expenditure in Britain the protagonists became known as navalists and anti-navalists, expressions whose modern equivalents are 'hawks' and 'doves'.

The key technical step in the arms race (akin to the introduction of the intercontinental ballistic missile or the MIRV) was the introduction, at Fisher's inspiration, of the Dreadnought. The features of the Dreadnought were that it was the first big ship in any navy to have turbine engines which could produce sustained high speeds with little maintenance; it could go faster than previous ships; and it was armed with a battery of ten twelve-inch guns and no secondary armament, apart from light quick-firing guns to repel torpedo attack. This armament meant that the weight of broadside it could produce was much larger than that of battleships of previous vintages. The launching of the world's largest, fastest, most powerful battleship in February 1906 by Kind Edward VII was a great public event, preceded and surrounded by much speculation as to the technical capabilities of the new ship.

The introduction of the Dreadnought was criticised on the grounds that, by rendering all existing battleships obsolete, it destroyed Britain's superiority in battleships of earlier vintages – a superiority which, *vis-à-vis* Germany, amounted to about 3 to 1. Since Germany would be able quickly to copy what Britain had done, a race would start in which the two sides started almost equal.

> Fisher never denied that the introduction of the *Dreadnought* was tantamount to starting *de novo*, since the vessel, in his opinion, was equal to any two and a half battleships then existing. But he was certain that the all-big-gun battleship was inevitable, on both technical grounds and on intelligence of what other powers were planning...[21]

There followed the race in battleship-building between Britain and Germany which displays the features of the arms race that we have seen about us since 1945. Here, it seems, is the period when the mould of the modern arms race was cast.

On the German side the objective was spelt out in a memorandum attached to the Navy Bill for an enlarged building programme. The memorandum enunciated Tirpitz's 'risk theory', according to which the German battle fleet did not have to be as strong as the British fleet; it had only to be strong enough to leave Britain vulnerable to other naval powers, meaning France and Germany, who were then potential enemies of Britain. This would mean that Britain would not wish to risk a confrontation with the German fleet but would prefer to make concessions to Germany in the colonial field. He recognised that as the German fleet grew, there would be a 'danger zone' when it would be vulnerable to a preventative attack by Britain – though in 1909 when the German Chancellor, von Bulow, expressed fears of war and sought to moderate Germany's naval programme, Tirpitz refused to admit the possibility of war on the grounds that the British were in no mood to fight.[22]

In practice, Britain, faced by the German challenge, improved her relations with France and Russia, with the result that Germany had to aim higher, at the progressive achievement of parity with Britain.

The British policy objective was 'the two-power standard' which dated back to the Earl of Chatham (1770) and, having been rediscovered after the Crimean War, was adopted as official policy by the First Lord of the Admiralty in 1889 when he stated that the idea underlying the speeches of all First Lords and Prime Ministers had been, 'that our establishment should be on such a scale that it should at least be equal to the naval strength of any two countries'.[23] As the risk of other major naval powers being enemies, and the pressure of the arms race increased, Britain abandoned the two-power standard in 1909 and adopted instead the standard of 60 per cent superiority in Dreadnoughts over Germany. This change in policy was secretly made in 1909, but was first made public only in 1912 when Churchill had become First Sea Lord.[24]

The race was concentrated on battleships of the new Dreadnought type, though battle cruisers using the new technology figured too. Its course was determined in great debates over the naval programmes and budgets. Up to the end of 1905 the British position seemed secure. The growth of the Fleet was satisfying the two-power standard with a margin of 10 per cent to spare, measured against Germany and Russia or France and Russia: the United States was regarded as friendly, and Japan, having been defeated by the Russians, was ignored too. But in 1906 the Liberals had come to power keen to save money for purposes of social reform and to set an example in international arms reduction. There was a 'Big Navy' wing of the party, led by Asquith, Grey and Haldane, which defeated the small navy wing led by Campbell-Bannerman and, after his death in 1908, by Lloyd George and Churchill. The Big Navy campaign played on fear of German Dreadnoughts. Initially there was some easing of the British ship-building programme, but then the failure of the second Hague Conference was followed by the Naval Scare of 1908–9. At the beginning of 1909 the prospect was that on present building programmes the Germans in 1912 would have thirteen dreadnought-type ships (battleships and battle cruisers of the new technology) whilst Britain would have eighteen. This looked weak compared with the traditions of the two-power standard which was still publicly embraced, but, more important than that, the Admiralty were seized by the false fear that the Germans were going to accelerate their programme to the point where they would certainly have seventeen and possibly twenty-one by the spring of 1913.[25]

The episode is so like the scares over the 'bomber gap' and the 'missile gap' in the nuclear arms race that it could appropriately be re-named the 'Dreadnought Gap'. The alarmist projections of what the Germans might produce were based on evidence that Germany's ship-building capacity and her capacity to manufacture guns and gun mountings had been greatly increased, and that she was secretly accumulating unusually large amounts of nickel, a material required for the making of armour.

There followed a great debate in Parliament and in the country. Navalists fought between the parties and within the ruling Liberal party. The Press took sides passionately, as did the Navy League and other pressure groups. And in the 'Mulliner affair', there was controversy over the part played by Mr Mulliner, the Managing Director of Coventry Ordinance Works, a new armament firm owned by three large ship-building firms, in spreading alarming information about the expansion of German capacity, in particular at Krupps, the maker of guns and gun mountings.[26]

The key issue in the debate was how many battleships should be provided for in the expenditure Estimates for the coming year, 1909–10, in order to ensure an acceptable naval position in 1912. Within the Liberal government the argument was over four or six; the Conservative opposition was calling for six. In the end the Government adopted the curious compromise of going for four, plus four extra ships (to be laid down not later than the end of the financial year) if the evidence as to the growth of the future German fleet justified it. In the course of the affair, Metternich, the German Ambassador in London, offered his assurances that Germany would have only thirteen dreadnoughts in 1913. He was mistrusted and ignored. By then the fever was high. The popular cry was, 'We want eight and we won't wait'.

In the event the Germans did not accelerate their programme but suffered delay through introducing modifications to keep up with British technical innovations. In 1912, when they were meant to have had thirteen, or possibly seventeen, capital ships, they had only nine. The British too had suffered slippages and had fifteen. Churchill concluded:

Looking back on the voluminous papers on this controversy in the light of what actually happened, there can be no doubt whatever that, as far as the facts and figures were concerned . . . the gloomy Admiralty anticipations were in no respect fulfilled in the year 1912 . . . There were no secret German Dreadnoughts, nor had

Admiral Tirpitz made any untrue statement in respect of major construction.[27]

But Churchill later reflected that McKenna, the First Lord of the Admiralty, had been right in that, if the British programme had been smaller, the Royal Navy would not have had the rather bare margin of security that it enjoyed in the critical early months of the war.

From 1910 onwards the race continued, with Britain building five or six dreadnoughts a year, keeping her lead over the Germans. In 1911, after the Agadir Crisis, the Germans pushed ahead. They introduced a supplementary naval budget and declared their intention to go for a ratio *vis-à-vis* Britain of 2 to 3. There was an attempt at negotiation, led by Haldane, but the Germans demanded that Britain accept the 2 to 3 ratio in capital ships, and that it agree to be neutral in the event of war. The British made it clear that they would accelerate building if the Germans went ahead with their expanding programme and that they would not entertain a commitment to stand aside and be neutral. In the event, Germany did not push its enlarged programme to the full. Britain kept its lead. In presenting the 1913–14 estimate, Churchill, now at the Admiralty and a born-again navalist, in explaining his proposals, branded the arms race as sheer stupidity and proposed a naval holiday for a year – or what in modern terms would be called a 'freeze' for a year. This was rejected by Germany, 'both on the general principle that the idea is Utopian and unworkable' and because 'the interruption for a whole year of Naval construction would throw innumerable men on the pavement'.[28]

When war broke out in 1914 the battleships served only to neutralise one another. The British fleet, rather than taking the risky position of blockading the German coast close to (as the Germans had assumed they would), conducted a long-range blockade, blocking egress from the North Sea round the north of Scotland and through the Channel. The German fleet stayed in or near its bases. At Jutland the two fleets met rather inconclusively.

In the event, submarines were of vastly greater importance than was foreseen, except by a few visionaries.

The German view of the naval arms race has been described by a German historian as follows:

there is no denying the fact that the German fleet from the outset was a fighting machine, even though only for defensive measures against England. On each occasion when we had had to evade the possibility of a conflict with England from lack of naval auxiliaries

– in the Jameson Raid of 1895, the Samoa question in 1899, the tension during the Boer War, and during the war in the Far East – the conviction had grown on the Kaiser and the leaders of our navy that our fleet must be increased sufficiently to secure that it could no longer be treated by England as a *quantum négligeable*. Since the Morocco crisis in 1905 the possibility of a naval war with England, little as we desired it, seemed to come closer every moment. We felt bound to be armed to meet it.[29]

The Disarmament Movement

In reaction to the tide of militarism there grew up in the latter part of the nineteenth century an anti-war movement which campaigned for the limitation of armaments. It consisted principally of liberals, socialists and members of non-conformist religious groups, but its aims gained some support from people all over the political spectrum. Another group within the broad movement were those who believed the strengthening of international law was the way to avoid war and who advocated, in particular, the use of arbitration to settle international disputes.

In 1889 the movement, 'which had manifested itself in numerous isolated resolutions on peace, arbitration and disarmament. . . became united in a common effort. . . through the organisation of two international peace bodies: the Universal Peace Congresses and the Inter-Parliamentary Union'.[30] With its two main planks, disarmament and arbitration, the movement gained a significant following amongst the liberal–radical élites and the sects from which its inspiration came. It no doubt helped to cause political leaders to pay lip service to disarmament. But the movement did not sway the bulk of public opinion, and in one of the main powers, Russia, no peace society existed and all peace propaganda was censored. A study of the movement for disarmament concluded:

In short, in 1898 there existed in England, the United States, and to a lesser extent in France and Germany, an inchoate opinion in favour of a limitation of arms, but this opinion did not exert a great influence upon governments. At the close of the century it was beginning to affect statesmen only in what they said, not in what they did.[31]

The Hague Conferences

The first inter-governmental conference to discuss disarmament in peacetime was the Hague conference of 1899, convened at the initiative of the Tsar of Russia. He appeared to be motivated by idealism, though considerations of economy and national interest can be traced too.[32]

The proposal was conveyed out of the blue on 24 August 1898, when, at the regular weekly meeting of the diplomatic representatives at St Petersburg, the Russian Foreign Minister, Count Muraviev, presented to each of the representatives a document, known as the 'Rescript'. It set a pattern for all the documents urging disarmament that have been produced in the subsequent ninety years. With a little amendment, the text could be used today. It reads as follows:

The maintenance of general peace, and a possible reduction of the excessive armaments which weigh upon all nations, present themselves in the existing condition of the whole world, as the ideal towards which the endeavours of all Governments should be directed.

The humanitarian and magnanimous ideas of His Majesty the Emperor, my August Master, have been won over to this view. In the conviction that this lofty aim is in conformity with the most essential interests and the legitimate views of all Powers, the Imperial Government thinks that the present moment would be very favourable for seeking, by means of international discussion, the most effectual means of insuring to all peoples the benefits of a real and durable peace, and, above all, of putting an end to the progressive development of the present armaments.

In the course of the last twenty years the longings for a general appeasement have become especially pronounced in the consciences of civilized nations. The preservation of peace has been put forward as the object of international policy; in its name great States have concluded between themselves powerful alliances; it is the better to guarantee peace that they have developed, in proportions hitherto unprecedented, their military forces, and still continue to increase them without shrinking from any sacrifice.

All these efforts nevertheless have not yet been able to bring about the beneficent results of the desired pacification. The financial charges following an upward march strike at the public prosperity at its very source.

The intellectual and physical strength of the nations, labour and capital, are for the major part diverted from their natural application, and unproductively consumed. Hundreds of millions are devoted to acquiring terrible engines of destruction, which, though to-day regarded as the last word of science, are destined to-morrow to lose all value in consequence of some fresh discovery in the same field.

National culture, economic progress, and the production of wealth are either paralyzed or checked in their development. Moreover, in proportion as the armaments of each Power increase so do they less and less fulfill the object which the Governments have set before themselves.

The economic crisis, due in great part to the system of armaments *à l'outrance*, and the continual danger which lies in this massing of war material, are transforming the armed peace of our days into a crushing burden, which the peoples have more and more difficulty in bearing. It appears evident, then, that if this state of things were prolonged, it would inevitably lead to the very cataclysm which it is desired to avert, and the horrors of which make every thinking man shudder in advance.

To put an end to these incessant armaments and to seek the means of warding off the calamities which are threatening the whole world – such is the supreme duty which is to-day imposed on all States.

Filled with this idea, His Majesty has been pleased to order me to propose to all the Governments whose representatives are accredited to the Imperial Court, the meeting of a conference which would have to occupy itself with this grave problem.

This conference should be, by the help of God, a happy presage for the century which is about to open. It would converge in one powerful focus the efforts of all States which are sincerely seeking to make the great idea of universal peace triumph over the elements of trouble and discord.

It would, at the same time, confirm their agreement by the solemn establishment of the principles of justice and right, upon which repose the security of States and the welfare of peoples.[33]

Whilst the invited states politely accepted the invitation and went to the Hague, their reactions were cynical. The Kaiser declared, 'I'll go along with the conference comedy but I'll keep my dagger at my side during the waltz' and later went even further: 'I agree to the stupid idea so that the Tsar doesn't look a fool in front of Europe. But I will in practice in future only rely on and trust God and my sword! And [expletive] on all the resolutions'.[34] 'The British War Office said much the same thing in more diplomatic language'.[35]

It was suggested at the time that Russia was calling for the limitation of arms only because she was feeling the pinch of keeping up in the arms race, and secondly, that she was calling for the limitation of the size of the armed forces but no limitation on the building of railways, in which she was behind.

The delegates sent by governments to the Conference included formidable people who had little sympathy for disarmament, for example, from the United States, Captain Mahan, the great advocate of seapower, and for Britain, Sir John Fisher, who, as we have seen, was later to be the driving force on the British side of the naval arms race.

By the time the Conference was convened, the items on the agenda included the use of arbitration to settle international disputes as well as the limitation of arms. The Conference divided into committees where, amongst proposals discussed, was a Russian detailed proposal for a freeze on armies, in terms of men and budgets, for five years and a naval freeze for three years specified in terms of budgets, tonnage and manpower. This is probably the first time the notion of a negotiated freeze was put forward. The Conference ended by establishing the Hague Court, a useful permanent court to which international disputes could be taken for arbitration, and some conventions relating to the rules of war. These conventions, to which not all the participating countries subscribed, banned in particular the use of expanding bullets and the use of asphyxiating gases.

As regards the level of arms, all that could be agreed was that, 'The Conference is of the opinion that the restriction of military charges, which are at present a heavy burden on the world, is extremely desirable for the increase of the material and moral welfare of mankind'.[36]

The failure to make more progress has been explained in the following terms:

First, difficult issues were raised which have plagued disarmament initiatives ever since 1899. Technical problems such as definition of weapons and verification controls became insurmountable for the Hague Conference delegates. . . Furthermore, without an example of the tremendous carnage of war, as would occur within fifteen years, public opinion supporting arms limitation proved only lukewarm. Finally, in an age of extreme nationalism, no country wanted really to give up. . . its complete freedom of action on the armaments issue.[37]

The Second Hague Conference in 1907, backed enthusiastically by the United States, again achieved no disarmament. It produced some further slight additions to the laws of war, including a ban for five years on aerial bombardment from balloons.

The interest of these conferences, the first of which took place ninety years ago, is that in them we see an early manifestation of problems that are still with us, in particular, the expression of national policies for and against arms limitation through technical arguments about definitions and verification.

B.   INTER-WAR NEGOTIATIONS

The Background

The background to arms negotiations in the inter-war period is very different from that in the period before 1914.

The slaughter in the trenches and the experience of total war produced a powerful reaction against war. By 1918 the populations and economic resources of industrialised nations had been mobilised on a scale never before contemplated, and the war was being fought by every means that was technically possible, including chemical warfare, naval blockade and aerial bombardment of cities – admittedly in rudimentary form compared with what was to come. Part of the reaction to the war was a new popular concern with international politics and popular support for pacifism.

The idea of a new international order based on the rule of law, which was strongly espoused by British and American liberals, found expression in the creation of the League of Nations as part of the peace settlement concluded at Versailles in 1919.

Another ingredient of the Versailles Treaty was the application to Europe of President Wilson's principle of self-determination, the main result of which was to split up the Austro–Hungarian empire.

A third ingredient, quite at odds with the liberal nature of the first two, was the imposition on Germany of a punitive peace. One of the key features of the peace settlement was the War Guilt Clause under

which Germany was made to accept blame and responsibility for all
loss and damage to the Allied nations; she was made to surrender all
her colonies and merchant fleet, and to commit herself to pay huge
financial reparations to the allies. The principle of self-determination
was not applied to Germany where it would have been to her
advantage (in Austria and the Sudetenland), whilst she was made to
cede bits of territory to Belgium, France, Czechoslovakia and
Poland; and Germany was forcibly disarmed whilst other countries
incurred only a moral obligation to disarm. Altogether Germany lost
13.5 per cent of her territory, 10 per cent of her population, besides
all her colonies, her armed forces and all her merchant ships over
1,600 ton, and she was made to promise to pay vast reparations.[38]
There is little wonder that Germans argued that the ending of
reparations and discriminatory disarmament were needed as a means
of easing unemployment or that the rejection of the Treaty became a
central element in the progamme on which Hitler campaigned for
office.

The United States, having been the most powerful and internationalist nation at the peace conference, reverted to isolation and failed
to join the League. The Soviet Union, run by revolutionaries who
appeared, whatever they said, to threaten the established order in
other countries, was treated more or less as an outcast, though she
was eventually let into the League in 1934.

This left Britain and France in a dominant position in Europe.
Their combined conduct would determine whether there would be
war or peace in Europe. France, having been savaged repeatedly by
Germany, and conscious that her population was being progressively
outnumbered by the Germans, was fearful of Germany and unwilling
to disarm, unless she obtained guarantees of security, meaning strong
commitments from her former allies that if she were attacked they
would intervene on her side. These she could not obtain. American
isolationism meant that no United States government could offer a
guarantee of that kind. Britain's first concern was the need to defend
her empire and her spheres of influence abroad, which had been
substantially enlarged at the end of the war by the acquisition of
ex-German possessions and by the acquisition of new spheres of
influence in the Middle East where the Ottoman empire had col-
lapsed. Secondly, extreme financial stringency, which was the order
of the day, meant that the British military authorities felt the need to
limit, not expand, commitments. Thirdly, there was a fear of giving
an excessive commitment to France. There appear to have been two
elements to this. One was the fear of making France too adventurous.

After the Peace Treaty and the failure of the United States to join the League of Nations, France, finding herself alone on the Continent now that she had lost the support of Russia through the interposition of the new Poland and the effects of the Revolution, was at first quite belligerent. She, together with Belgium, occupied the Ruhr in 1923 on the grounds that Germany had defaulted on her reparations deliveries of coal and timber. And before that relations between Britain and France had deteriorated sharply.[39]

Another explanation offered for Britain's reluctance to make military commitments to go to the aid of France is that Britain was afraid that France was trying to pass to her the burden of Continental defence. In colloquial terms, there was 'buck-passing' between Britain and France, with France trying to get Britain to share the burden of Continental defence, and Britain holding back.[40]

The Approach to Disarmament

After the 1914–18 war disarmament was treated not as a matter of half measures. It meant the reduction of armed forces down to minimal levels, in association with agreement to outlaw war and to settle disputes by non-military means. Since 1945 these aims may have seemed idealistic, their attainment remote – though they have lived on in the shadows because they offer a vision of a world where nations live in harmony and order, a vision that people can grasp and put in place of the prevailing notion that nations can co-exist only in a state of anarchy, competing in arms, singly or in alliances, and restrained only by mutual threats. That vision underlay the pursuit of disarmament after 1918.

The nations engaged in the making of the peace settlement made two rather equivocal commitments to engage in the pursuit of disarmament. The preamble to the Treaty of Versailles said that the disarmament of Germany was imposed 'in order to render possible the initiation of a general limitation of the armaments of all nations', a proposition which, together with a gloss upon it in an Allied communication to the Germans in June 1919, implied a moral obligation on the Allies to disarm. Secondly, Article 8 of the Covenant of the League of Nations called on the Council of the League to draw up disarmament plans 'for the consideration and action of the several Governments'.[41]

The climax came with the World Disarmament Conference of 1932 and it was at this conference that the qualitative approach to disarmament, with which we are particularly concerned, was adopted. But before that progress was made with naval disarmament.

Naval Disarmament

The pre-1914 'high-tech' arms race had its focus at sea. Battleships were the most sophisticated and conspicuous machines of war that man had ever developed. Attention was focused on the relative numbers and the characteristics of the battleships possessed by Britain and Germany. Battleships were the equivalent of the long-range ballistic missile today.

After the 1914–18 war, in which battleships of the two sides had held one another in check and had been engaged in large-scale battle only once, rather inconclusively at Jutland, the German fleet was at the bottom of the sea; at Scapa Flow, its commanders had scuttled the fleet rather than surrender it intact. The largest remaining fleets were those of Britain and the United States. Japan's fleet was a third force to be reckoned with. The core question was whether there would be Anglo-American naval competition. This was avoided when a naval agreement limiting capital ships was reached in Washington in 1922. Even though the two strongest participants in the conference were more friendly than antagonistic to each other, the agreement was quite an achievement. France, Japan and Italy were parties to the Treaty, as well as Britain and the United States. It was an encouraging first step in the realm of disarmament; but submarines, light cruisers and auxiliaries were not covered by the agreement, principally owing to the opposition of France, ever concerned with her security. After further negotiations in the 1920s, a further naval agreement was reached in London in 1930 between Britain, Japan and the United States, but rivalry between France and Italy prevented these two countries from engaging in any new undertakings; and Germany now began to circumvent the limits on what warships she was allowed to possess by building 'pocket battleships'.[42]

General Disarmament

General disarmament was pursued in Geneva, though it was also pursued regionally. For example, a treaty for the mutual reduction of arms was concluded in 1923 between five republics of Central America – Guatemala, Honduras, Salvador, Nicaragua and Costa Rica;[43] and in 1922 a conference was held in Moscow between the Soviet Union and its Eastern European neighbours on the disarmament of that area.[44] In Geneva, the League established a permanent military commission of professionals who were, 'more easily impressed by the difficulties than the urgency of reducing armaments'.[45] Although they were not members of the League, the United States and the Soviet Union joined in the negotiations in Geneva which were appended to the formal organisation of the League.

In the 1920s discussion focused on quantitative disarmament, i.e. the reduction of the general level of armaments, not upon the reduction or elimination of offensive weapons. Little was achieved.

A preparatory commission began work in November 1930 for the World Disarmament Conference, to be held in 1932. The preparatory commission swiftly became enmeshed in the problems of measuring the relative strength of different nations. This is exactly the same as the problem of measuring the military balance discussed in Chapters 2 and 5. From these debates, three points concerning the technical problems of disarmament may be of interest today:

First, there were long wrangles over the meaning of 'effectives', i.e. the number of effective soldiers, sailors and airmen. How much training made a soldier an effective? What was to be done about reserves? At what stage did they cease to be effectives? Further, it was argued that, if troops only had a short period of training, say six months, they would be suitable for defensive fighting, whereas if they had a longer period of training and constituted a more professional army, they would be suitable for offensive fighting. A notion of offensiveness and defensiveness crept into the problem of counting effectives.

Secondly, there was no agreement on the question of how to limit navies – whether by total tonnage or by numbers of different categories of warship – battleships, cruisers, destroyers, submarines and so on.

Thirdly, when it came to the limitation of military equipment, then usually termed 'war matériel', it was concluded that equipment was so varied and difficult to compare that, rather than attempt to legislate by reference to types of equipment, it would be better to set budgetary limits and leave countries to choose what types of equipment they bought. The feasibility of budgetary control was explored by experts.

Qualitative Disarmament

It was at the end of these rather unsatisfactory discussions of quantitative disarmament that in 1932 qualitative disarmament came to the fore as an alternative approach.[46] The banning of selected weapons figured in discussion of quantitative disarmament in the 1920s, having already been incorporated in the Treaty of Versailles, under which Germany was forbidden to possess military and naval aircraft, chemical weapons, armoured cars, tanks and guns of a calibre greater than 104 mm. But before 1932 the weapons appear to have been singled out as candidates for abolition not directly by a criterion of offensiveness as distinct from defensiveness, but because they were the most modern and destructive means of warfare. Thus Philip Noel-Baker in 1926 argued that as part of a general disarmament treaty it would be desirable 'to abolish some at least of the more costly and dangerous types of weapon and to limit the permitted size of others', and he discussed submarines, warships, military aircraft, tanks, artillery and chemical weapons as candidates for abolition or limitations.[47]

Like most ideas, qualitative disarmament, meaning the removal of offensive weapons, has many parents. One person who has made a poignant claim to paternity is Liddell Hart. In his memoirs he describes how in May 1931 he was consulted by Sir Samuel Hoare, a Conservative politician, on behalf of an all-party committee about how to approach disarmament at the coming Disarmament Conference. Having studied the problem, Liddell Hart concluded that the problem of agreeing on numerical balance in arms was an insuperable obstacle to the quantitative approach.

The more I studied the problem the more clearly I came to see that it was *qualitative* rather than *quantitative* – the root of it lying in the kind of weapons which inherently favoured the offensive. If an international agreement could be attained for their universal abolition, there could be a real chance of nullifying the prospects of successful aggression.

It was the hardest test that ever confronted me in striving to take a completely objective view. . . For I soon realised that the obvious solution would entail annulling not only the development of tanks as a military tool but the whole concept of reviving the power of the offensive and the art of war, by 'lightning' strokes with highly mobile mechanised forces – thus cancelling out all I had done during the past ten years to develop and preach this new military concept. . . it would mean strangling my 'own baby'.[48]

Another person to whom the idea of qualitative disarmament, meaning the removal of offensive weapons, can be traced is Lord Robert Cecil, one of the architects of the League of Nations who devoted his life to the cause of peace and disarmament. He sets out the case for this approach, and describes his adoption of it, in a passage of his memoirs which appears to refer to a date earlier than that given by Liddell Hart.[49] Whatever the origins of the idea of qualitative disarmament, it was put forward at the begining of the Geneva Disarmament Conference in February 1932 by Lord Robert Cecil.[50] The idea was supported by the United States delegate and others, and the Conference agreed to appoint three Technical Commissions on Land, Naval and Air armaments respectively, to undertake the task of defining offensive weapons. They were appointed by the General Commission of the Conference in March 1932. On 22 April 1932 the General Commission instructed them to examine 'the range of land, sea and air armaments. . . with a view to selecting those weapons whose character is the most specifically offensive, or those most efficacious against national defence or most threatening to civilians'.[51] The results of the work of the technical commissions were these:[52]

(a) The Naval Commission disagreed hopelessly over what type of ship, if any, was offensive, with the member nations essentially taking positions that fitted their national interest. For example, the United States and Britain said no ships were offensive, but they supported the abolition of submarines; the weaker powers supported the abolition of big ships (which they could not afford).

(b) The Land Commission seems to have had no difficulty in focussing on tanks and large guns as offensive types of weapon, but they disagreed on definitions. The French and British said that only large tanks were offensive. The French favoured abolishing tanks over 70 tons, since they were experimenting with a tank of that remarkable size. The British, who were experimenting with 16 ton tanks, went for a limit of 25 tons. In the end the Commission agreed on a limit of 70 tons. Others argued that all armoured fighting vehicles, including armoured cars, should be abolished.

(c) The Air Commission was scarcely able to get beyond truisms, saying, for example that any aeroplane might be used for military purposes and that bombing was bad. There was a proposal to bring civil airlines under international control or international ownership.

There was a special committee on chemical and bacteriological weapons, which could be used by air, land or naval forces. It was practically unanimous in proposals for the abolition of these weapons.

The Survey of International Affairs for 1932, produced at the Royal Institute of International Affairs in London under the direction of Arnold Toynbee, summed up as follows:

On the technical side, the position of the Disarmament Conference after four months' work was that, except in the case of chemical and bacteriological methods, the 'qualitative' line of approach, which had seemed to offer such hopeful possibilities as a short-cut to disarmament, was blocked by the inability of the experts to agree.[53]

In order to try to break the deadlock and show initiative in the year of a Presidential Election, President Hoover, through his representative in Geneva, Mr Gibson, in June 1932 put forward a specific plan for qualitative disarmament which attempted to cut through the problem of definitions, as well as reassuring France in its quest for security. He argued that the Kellogg Pact already said that arms should be used for defence only and that to increase the comparative power of defence through decreases in the power of attack would improve security.[54] He therefore called for cuts in armies by one third and proposed specifically the following qualitative changes: abolish all tanks, chemical and bacteriological weapons and large field guns;

abolish all 'bombing planes'; and start on naval negotiations where the Washington and London Treaties had left off.[55]

The responses to this proposal were as much political as technical. France was negative, asking what the United States would do in the event of a breach of the Kellogg Pact, i.e. in the event of somebody going to war offensively. The United States could not reassure France on this point. Britain said the naval proposals were unacceptable; Britain would not abolish all tanks; and she must consult the members of the Commonwealth. More figures for the size of tanks and the limit to the size of guns were bandied about but the nature of the debate did not change.

By now the Conference had run into the sands. Germany under Brüning had pleaded that she must be granted equality of treatment if Hitler was to be prevented from coming to power. Brüning's successor, von Papen, made a last effort, offering France a customs union and military staff arrangements in return for an end to economic reparations and equality of rights for German armaments, but the offer was rejected. Von Papen abandoned any pretence at an internationalist policy and in September 1932 withdrew from the Disarmament Conference. In January 1933 Hitler came to power.

The Soviet Union, when it joined the disarmament discussions in 1927, adopted a fundamentalist position with a grand scheme for general disarmament and took a similar position on qualitative disarmament, maintaining, for example, that all tanks were offensive weapons. Sceptics in the West, for example Madariaga, argued that the Soviet Union wanted military disarmament because it conquered by other means, namely revolution.[56]

A view of the Conference was offered at the time by Allen Dulles, who had been at the Paris Peace conference and was a member of the United States Delegation to the Disarmament Conference. (Later he was to become head of the United States Central Intelligence Agency.) He observed that 'the extreme difficulty of fixing numerical limits led the Conference to seize upon the idea of qualitative disarmament', and went on to say that, 'The first and certainly one of the important results of the Geneva Conference was thus the acceptance of the principle of qualitative disarmament and the agreement to apply it to heavy guns, tanks and military aviation'. He argued that 'France held the key to disarmament on land and in the air. With her allies she dominated the military situation of Europe'; and also that 'qualitative disarmament helps to provide security'. Altogether he was rather positive about qualitative disarmament.[57]

The Lessons

To assess the lessons of these early arms negotiations, it is helpful to go back to first principles. Strategy is the art of pursuing political aims by the use or possession of military means. Arms negotiations, which influence the quantity and quality of arms possessed by you and your neighbours, are one means of implementing strategy. It follows that progress to reduce arms will be made only when the parties to a negotiation have peaceful aims and for that purpose seek arms reductions as part of their military strategy.

It follows that the first question to consider is, were these conditions met in the two periods under examination?

It is pretty clear that for the period before 1914 the answer is no. Germany's aims were scarcely peaceful, and she and most of the other main powers at the Hague Conferences were opposed to arms reductions and sought strong offensive forces.

The answer for the inter-war period is more complex. The failure of disarmament negotiations was part of the larger failure of the leading nations, first and foremost the United States, to support the League of Nations and build a new security system within its framework; and it was a consequence of the half-Carthaginian peace imposed on Germany, under the provisions of which she was punished, disarmed and humiliated, but her power to recover and strike back was not permanently destroyed, nor was she allowed to resume her place on a par with others with respect to the arms she was allowed to possess and other matters. In this setting, political aims amongst the war-shattered nations may generally have been peaceful, but those aims found expression, notably on the part of France, in a desire to remain free to build up arms against Germany rather than in a willingness to disarm down to the level of Germany; and once Hitler had come to power, the common ground of peaceful political aims, such as it was, was gone.

The second point is that the setting in which qualitative disarmament was pursued in the inter-war years was very different from that which we face today. Now, two alliances face each other heavily armed with nuclear and non-nuclear weapons, although their political differences have faded. A military rapprochement between them requires the adoption of less offensive strategies; and the implementation of those strategies requires an approach which combines independent actions, consultation and negotiation.

The inter-war approach was part of the attempt to build a new international order in which the rule of law would govern relations between many nations as it governed relations between individuals within a nation state. That was the spirit and ideal which infused the Paris Peace Conference, the Treaty of Versailles, and the League of Nations. It was taken for granted that the way to achieve results was by the negotiation of international agreements, by law-making. With the Treaty of Versailles as a model, attention was concentrated on the problems of defining the level of forces and then the problems of picking out the least desirable kinds of weapons.

The result was that when it came to qualitative disarmament there was little or no analysis of the merits of defensive strategies or of the alternative ways of implementing them, including unilateral change. There was an immediate plunge into haggling and bargaining in which arguments about definition of offensive weapons became an expression of political positions as much as of technical problems.

The third point to note is that in the attempt to define offensive weapons there was a failure at the 1932 Conference, and in the surrounding debate amongst experts, to distinguish clearly between one-sided and two-sided (or many-sided) removal of offensive weapons. There is a vital distinction between the questions:

1. Can this weapon in any circumstances help an offensive? To which answer is always yes: even a minefield can help an offensive by releasing troops from defensive duties to join an attack.
2. Would this weapon, if removed from both sides, reduce the chances of either being able to attack successfully? To which the answer will sometimes be yes, sometimes no.

It is the second question that is relevant to qualitative disarmament. A good example of failure clearly to make this distinction is an exchange in 1931 and 1932 in the *English Review* between Fuller and Liddell Hart, two of the great military experts of the time.

Fuller argued that 'all weapons must of their very nature be aggressive, consequently the problem resolves itself into degrees of aggression'; that to abolish modern mechanised weapons would drive one back to more primitive weapons; and that this led him to fear that 'A time may come when there is another war, and nothing will be more pitiful to us generals than to see thousands of our men slaughtered in cold blood, because the very means which would mitigate this slaughter have been denied us in the name of peace and humanity'.[58]

Liddell Hart replied that Fuller was expressing a soldier's desire to be assured of the weapons to win a war should it occur, whereas the problem of statesmen in Geneva was to prevent war. In the 1914–1918 war,

> The only means whereby the attack was enabled to make partial headway. . . was by the use, first, of an overwhelming mass of heavy artillery, and second, by the use of tanks. . . The point of the qualitative principle is not that certain weapons are in themselves more offensive than others, but that they alone make it possible under certain conditions to make a decisive offensive against a neighbouring country. Abolish such weapons by argument, and there would be little chance of successful aggression – and so a real discouragement to any would-be aggressor.[59]

Liddell Hart's argument, which refers to abolition, is clearly about the multilateral abolition of offensive weapons; Fuller's argument seems to slide from one concept to the other; and neither addresses the point that what weapons you need for defence (or offence) depends on what weapons your opponent possesses.

The lesson is that you must pose the right question – the second of the two posed above. If you ask experts to categorise weapons, forces, training, deployments or logistics as offensive (or defensive) in general terms of universal application, it is predictable that you will run into a treacherous bog. As Liddell Hart put it in 1932,

> the technical experts at Geneva have recently been 'sapping' the principle of qualitative disarmament. . . by concentrating on the term 'offensive weapons', and on the mere letter instead of the spirit. Naturally all weapons can be called 'offensive' – in the sense they can inflict injury on the body of an enemy! And all weapons can be useful to the defence as well as to the attack. This fact is so obvious that one would wonder at the expenditure of breath in discussing it, were it not so palpably a smoke-screen round the whole issue.[60]

Notes and References

1 Introduction

1. **Karl von Clausewitz,** *On War*, Col J. J. Graham (trans.) (London, 1940).
2. In 1955, Bernard Brodie, the most far-sighted of post-war American strategic theorists, discussing the advent of thermo-nuclear weapons, to the explosive power of which there is no upper limit, wrote 'This. . . brings us, in short, to the end of strategy as we have known it' (Bernard Brodie, 'Strategy Hits a Dead End', *Harper's* (October 1955), cited in Gregg Herken, *Counsels of War* (New York: Knopf, 1985) p. 38. Lawrence Freedman, a leading British military historian, after a 400-page study, *The Evolution of Nuclear Strategy* (London: Macmillan, 1981), concluded with the words, 'C'est magnifique, mais ce n'est pas la stratégie' (p. 400). Robert Jervis, an American political theorist, concluded his book on nuclear strategy by saying, 'We will have to find new and different paths', *The Illogic of American Nuclear Strategy* (Ithaca, NY: Cornell University Press, 1984) p. 170.
3. Major-General J. W. Stainer, in *A Conventional Strategy for the Central Front in NATO – Report of a Seminar held at the Royal United Services Institute for Defence Studies* (London: RUSI, June 1975) p. 16.

2 The Political Level

1. Bernard Brodie, *The Absolute Weapon: Atomic Power and World Order* (New York: Harcourt Brace, 1946) p. 76.
2. B.H. Liddell Hart, *History of the First World War* (London: Pan Books, 1972) p.22.
3. For a western definition of doctrine and discussion of its meaning, see Barry R. Posen, *The Sources of Military Doctrine: France, Britain and Germany Between the Wars* (Ithaca and London: Cornell University Press, 1984).
4. *Soviet Military Encyclopaedia, 1976*, cited in Gerard Holden, *ADIU Report*, Vol. 9, No. 6 (November–December 1987).
5. Alexei Arbatov, 'Military Doctrines', Chapter 11, *Disarmament and Security, 1987 Yearbook* (Moscow, USSR: Institute of World Economy and International Relations, Novosti Press Agency Publishing House, 1988) p.201; and Christopher N. Donnelly, 'Soviet Approaches to Arms Control, *Bulletin of the Council for Arms Control*, No. 41 (December 1988) (Oxford: Brassey's).
6. The significance of defensive superiority was first expressed in formal terms like this by Anders Boserup in a series of papers, for example, 'Non-offensive Defence in Europe', in Derek Paul (ed.), *Defending Europe – Options for Security* (Philadelphia: Taylor & Francis, 1985).

7. Alfred Count von Schlieffen, Chief of the German General Staff, *Dienstschriften*, cited in Jehuda L. Wallach, *The Dogma of the Battle of Annihilation: The Theories of Clausewitz and Schlieffen and their Impact on the German Conduct of Two World Wars* (Westport, Conn. and London: Greenwood Press, 1986) p. 55.

3 The Nuclear Level

1. Consideration of relative non-nuclear strength will be germane to the decision of the nuclear country insofar as it must assess whether the non-nuclear nation could respond to a nuclear threat by taking territory or threatening to do so with its non-nuclear forces.
2. McGeorge Bundy, 'The Bishops and the Bomb', *New York Review of Books* (16 June 1983).
3. Anders Boserup, 'Beyond Deterrence: a Quiet Reminder', paper submitted to the 39th Pugwash Conference, Cambridge, Mass. (1989).
4. Thomas C. Schelling, in *The Strategy of Conflict* (Harvard University Press, 1960) was the first to try applying game theory to strategy and arms control, but in the preface to the 1980 edition he says that he had hoped 'I now think mistakenly, that the theory of games might be redirected toward application in these several fields' (p. vi). A discussion of the problem of applying game theory to strategy is to be found in Martin Shubik, 'On the study of disarmament and escalation', *Journal of Conflict Resolution*, Vol XII, No. 1 (1968).
5. Game Theory also yielded Prisoner's Dilemma, an analogy for the arms race. See Chapter 5.
6. Herman Kahn, *On Escalation: Metaphors and Scenarios* (London: Pall Mall Press, 1965) pp. 39, 290.
7. I am indebted to Catherine Bateson for this point and anecdote.
8. See Barry M. Blechman and Douglas M. Hart, 'The Political Utility of Nuclear Weapons: The 1973 Middle East Crises', *International Security*, Vol. 7, No. 1 (1982).
9. See Robert Jervis, *The Illogic of American Nuclear Strategy* (Ithaca NY: Cornell University Press, 1984) p. 31.
10. Kahn, *On Escalation*, p. 58.
11. For a discussion of the meaning of rationality in this context see Stephen Maxwell, *Rationality in Deterrence*, Adelphi Paper No. 50 (August 1968) The Institute For Strategic Studies, London, in particular, p. 7.
12. Jervis, *The Illogic of American Nuclear Strategy*, pp. 59, 130.
13. McGeorge Bundy, George Kennan, Robert McNamara and Gerard Smith, 'Nuclear Weapons and the Atlantic Alliance', *Foreign Affairs* (Spring 1982).

4 The Sub-nuclear Level

1. B. H. Liddell Hart, *Deterrent or Defence: A Fresh Look at the West's Military Position* (London: Stevens, 1960) p. 66.

2. See Heinz Brill, *Bogislav von Bonin im Spannungsfeld zwischen Wiederbewaffnung – Westintegration – Wiedervereinigung* (Baden-Baden, 1987).

3. Guy Brossollet, *Essai sur la Non-Bataille* (Paris: Editions Belin, 1975).

4. E. Spannocchi, 'Verteidigung ohne Selbstzerstörung' in C. F. von Weizsacker (ed.), *Verteidigung ohne Schlacht* (Munich, 1976).

5. H. Afheldt, *Verteidigung und Frieden: Politik mit Militärischen Mitteln* (Munich, 1976); and *Defensive Verteidigung* (Hamburg, 1983); and (a brief exposition by Afheldt of his ideas in English) 'Tactical Nuclear Weapons and European Security', in *Tactical Nuclear Weapons: European Perspectives*, SIPRI (London: Taylor & Francis, 1978).

6. See, for example, Lt Col. Norbert Hannig, 'The Defense of Western Europe with Conventional Weapons', *International Defense Review*, 11/1981, pp. 1439–43; J. Löser, *Weder Rot noch Tot–Überleben ohne Atomkrieg – Eine sicherheitspolitische Alternative* (München, 1982); or for an English version of Löser, 'The Security Network of an Area-Cover System for NATO', paper presented to the 1st Pugwash Study Group on Conventional Forces in Europe, 1984. For further examples, see Bjorn Moller, *Non-Offensive Defence: Bibliography*, Centre of Peace and Conflict Research at the University of Copenhagen.

7. See Mary Kaldor, *The Baroque Arsenal* (London: André Deutsch, 1982).

8. For a survey of the history of the relative strength of defence and offense, and an attempt to give the precise meaning to that concept, see Jack. S. Levy, 'The Offensive/Defensive Balance of Military Technology: A Theoretical and Historical Analysis', *International Studies Quarterly*, 28 (1984) pp. 219–38.

9. For a broad review of the prospects, see *Diminishing the Nuclear Threat – NATO's Defence and New Technology*, British Atlantic Council (London, February 1984).

10. F. W. Lanchester, *Aircraft in Warfare: The Dawn of the Fourth Arm* (London: Constable & Co., 1916) Chapter 5, 'The Principle of Concentration. The N-Square Law'.

11. See Robert Neild, 'The Implications of the Increasing Accuracy of Non-Nuclear Weapons', in Anders Boserup and Robert Neild (eds), *The Foundations of Defensive Defence* (London: Macmillan, 1990); and Anders Boserup, 'Military Stability and Defence Dominance: Elements of an Analytical Framework', in Boserup and Neild (eds), *The Foundations of Defensive Defence*.

12. See Liddell Hart, *Deterrent or Defence*, pp. 102–9.

13. See Dr Audrey Kokoshin and General V. Larionov, 'The Confrontation of Conventional Forces in the context of Ensuring Strategic Stability', in Neild and Boserup (eds), *The Foundations of Defensive Defence*.

14. Strategic bombing has in fact been rather unsuccessful. It has been resorted to on a large scale only by rich nations when they have been unable to bring their strength effectively to bear on their enemy in other ways, notably Britain and the United States against Germany and Japan in the Second World War, the United States against Korea and Vietnam, and the Soviet Union against Afghanistan.

15. See General Carlo Jean, 'Airpower and Conventional Stability', in Boserup and Neild (eds), *The Foundations of Defensive Defence*.

16. That for navies there can be no distinction between defence and attack was emphasised forcibly by Captain Mahan, the American naval historian and advocate of seapower. He asserted that coastal fortifications and other immobile, passive defences belonged to the army and 'everything that moves in the water to the navy, which has the prerogative of the offensive defence', Captain A. T. Mahan, *The Influence of Sea Power Upon History, 1660–1783* (London: Sampson Low, Marston & Co., 1892), note 1, p. 87.

17. For a general survey of the strategies of the European neutral nations see Adam Roberts, *Nations in Arms* (Chatto & Windus for the International Institute for Strategic Studies, London 1976).

18. Major General Gustav Daniker, *The Swiss Model of Conventional Defence*, Berne (April 1986) paper presented by Colonel General Gerhard Leu to the 11th IPRA Conference (Summer, 1987).

19. See SIPRI *Yearbook of World Armaments and Disarmament, 1988* (Oxford: Oxford University Press, 1988) pp. 168–9, and *The Military Balance 1987–1988* (London: IISS, 1987), pp. 215–17 and country sections.

20. Daniker, *The Swiss Model*, p. 11.

21. See Reiner K. Huber, *Some Remarks on Structural Implications of Strategic Stability in Central Europe*, paper presented to the 5th meeting of the Pugwash Study Group on Conventional Forces in Europe (October 1986); and H. W. Hofman, R. K. Huber and K. Steiner, 'On Reactive Defense Options – A Comparative Systems Analysis of Alternatives for the Initial Defense against the First Strategic Echelon of the Warsaw Pact in Central Europe', in Reiner K. Huber (ed.), *Modelling and Analysis of Conventional Defense in Europe* (New York and London, 1986).

22. John J. Mearsheimer, *Conventional Deterrence* (Cornell University Press, 1983) Chapter 2, in particular pp. 63–4.

23. Anders Boserup, 'Unilateral and Bilateral Approaches to Mutual Defensive Superiority: a Note on the Interplay of Stationary and Mobile Forces along an Extended Front', in Boserup and Neild (eds), *Foundations of Defensive Defence*.

24. For example, David Gates does not consider the two-sided case in his paper *Non-Offensive Defence: A Strategic Contradiction?* (Institute for European Defence and Strategic Studies, London, 1987).

25. See Anders Boserup, 'Military Stability and Defence Dominance: Elements of an Analytical Framework', in Boserup and Neild (eds), *The Foundations of Defensive Defence*.

26. Liddell Hart, *Deterrent or Defence*, pp. 108–9.

27. John J. Mearsheimer, 'Manoeuver, Mobile Defense and the NATO Central Front' *International Security*, Vol. 6, No. 3 (Winter 1981/1982) p. 120.

28. See Alan James, *The UN on Golan: Peacekeeping Paradox*, Norwegian Institute of International Affairs, Report No. 100 (January 1986).

5 The Implementation of a Strategy

1. The following discussion follows closely Robert Neild, 'The Case against Arms Negotiations and For a Reconsideration of Strategy', *Arms Control*, Vol. 7, No. 2 (September 1986).
2. I am indebted to Sir Rudolph Peierls for this point made during a discussion of these points.
3. Bernard Brodie, *Strategy in the Missile Age* (Princeton University Press, 1959) p. 174
4. Scott D. Sagan, '1914 Revisited: Allies, Offense and Instability', *International Security*, Vol. 11, No. 2 (Fall 1986) pp. 155–6.

6 Interpretation of the Period Since 1945

1. Horst Afheldt, 'The Necessity, Preconditions and Consequences of a No-First-Use Policy', paper submitted to the 45th Pugwash Symposium, Copenhagen (March 1984).
2. C. Rice, 'The Making of Soviet Strategy', in Peter Paret (ed.), *Makers of Modern Strategy from Machiavelli to the Nuclear Age* (Oxford: Oxford University Press, 1986) p. 654.
3. John Erickson, *The Soviet High Command: a military–political history 1918–1941* (London: Macmillan, 1962) p. 127.
4. Erickson, *The Soviet High Command*, p.129.
5. Raymond L. Garthoff, *How Russia Makes War: Soviet Military Doctrine* (London: George Allen & Unwin, 1954) p. 65.
6. Garthoff, *How Russia makes War*, p. 68.
7. Erickson, *The Soviet High Command*, p. 613.
8. Erickson, *The Soviet High Command*, p. 666.
9. Professor Patrick Blackett offered this explanation in 1962 in the following terms: 'as the Western nuclear strength grew, the Soviet Union gradually built up her land forces so as to be able to invade Europe even after an American nuclear attack – this was at that time their only possible military reply to the Western nuclear striking-power', P. M. S. Blackett, *Studies in War, Nuclear and Conventional* (London: Oliver & Boyd, 1962) p. 151.
   See Michael M. MccGuire, *Military Objectives in Soviet Foreign Policy*, Brookings Institution, Washington, D.C. (1987); and 'Rethinking War: The Soviets and European Security', *The Brookings Review* (Spring 1988).
11. Alexei Arbatov, 'Military Doctrines', Chapter 11, *Disarmament and Security, 1987 Yearbook* (Moscow, USSR: Institute of World Economy and International Relations, Novosti Press Agency Publishing House, 1988) p.210.
12. For short accounts of the evolution of western strategy after 1945 see Lawrence Freedman 'The First Two Generations of Nuclear Strategists' and Michael Carver 'Conventional Warfare in the Nuclear Age', both in Paret (ed.), *Makers of Modern Strategy from Machiavelli to the Nuclear Age*. For fuller accounts see Jane E. Stromseth, *The Origins of*

Flexible Response (Oxford: Macmillan Press, in association with St Anthony's College, 1988); and Lawrence Freedman, *The Evolution of Nuclear Strategy* (London: Macmillan, 1981).

13. NSC–162/2, quoted in Carver, 'Conventional Warfare', p. 782 and Stromseth, *The Origins of Flexibile Response*, p. 13.

14. General Maxwell Taylor, cited in Stromseth, *The Origins of Flexible Response*, p. 13.

15. Carver 'Conventional Warfare', pp. 782–3.

16. Stromseth, *The Origins of Flexible Response*, pp. 35–41.

17. The North Atlantic Treaty of 1949 was a treaty of the traditional type whereby a group of nations agreed to go to the help of any one of them which was attacked. NATO, formed in 1950, was a standing military organisation under an American supreme commander who, in the event of war, would automatically take command of the forces of member nations that had been committed to NATO in peacetime.

18. For a critical view, see Major T. Cross, 'Forward Defence – Time for a Change', *RUSI Journal* (June 1985) p. 19.

19. See Fabio Muni, 'Employment of Non-Mechanised Infantry for a Non-Provocative Defence', paper submitted to the 45th Pugwash Symposium, Copenhagen (March 1984) mimeo.

20. General John R. Galvin, 'The Continuing Validity of Flexible Response and Forward Defence', *RUSI Journal* (Summer, 1988) p. 8.

21. A similar view was expressed by McGeorge Bundy after he retired from the post of National Security Advisor to the President of the United States. See McGeorge Bundy, 'To Cap the Volcano', *Foreign Affairs* (October 1959).

22. See Gregg Herken, *Counsels of War* (New York: Knopf, 1985).

23. Desmond Ball, 'U.S. Strategic Forces: How would They Be Used?', *International Security*, Vol. 7, No. 3 (Winter 1982/1983) pp. 32–3.

24. See Oliver Ramsbotham, *Modernising NATO's Nuclear Weapons – No Decisions Have Been Made* (London: Macmillan, 1989).

25. See Marc Trachtenberg, 'A "Wasting Asset" – American Strategy and the Shifting Balance, 1949–1954', *International Security*, Vol.13, No.3 (Winter 1988/89).

26. NSC 68 quoted in Trachtenberg, 'A "Wasting Asset"', p. 13.

27. McGeorge Bundy, *Danger and Survival: Choices about the Bomb in the First Fifty Years* (New York: Random House, 1988) p. 229.

28. See Bundy, *Danger and Survival*, p. 321.

29. See Trachtenberg, 'A "Wasting Asset"', p. 40, and Bundy, *Danger and Survival*, p. 341.

30. Des Ball, 'U.S. Strategic Forces', p. 32.

31. The introduction of MIRVs (multiple independently-targetable re-entry vehicles) meant that with one ballistic missile you could aim warheads at a number of targets and so increase the probability that in a first strike you could 'disarm' your opponent by destroying his missiles.

32. See Dwight D. Eisenhower, *The White House Years: Waging Peace, 1956–1961* (New York: Doubleday, 1965) pp. 389–90, 547, footnote 1; and for a comment thereon, Bundy, *Danger and Survival*, p. 338.

33. For exposition of the use of the word deterrence in its wide sense, see John J. Mearsheimer, *Conventional Deterrence* (Cornell University Press, 1983) pp. 14–17.

34. See Steven Kull, 'Nuclear Nonsense', *Foreign Policy*, No. 58 (Spring 1985).

35. Steven Kull, 'Feeling good about hard-target-kill capability' (adapted from his forthcoming book, *Minds at War: Nuclear Reality and the Inner Conflicts of Defense Decisionmakers*) Bulletin of the Atomic Scientists (July/August 1988) p. 35.

36. See Arbatov, 'Military Doctrines', pp. 214–15.

37. That the negotiations were in the nature of a charade is illustrated by events in 1955. Britain and France persuaded the United States to join them in submitting some radical and quite balanced proposals for general disarmament. When the Soviet Union, unexpectedly, accepted them as a basis for negotiation, the United States withdrew its support for the proposals. In their place, President Eisenhower put forward the 'Open Skies' proposal at his summit meeting with Mr Khrushchev in Geneva later that year. It was not expected in the United States Government that the Soviet Union would accept Open Skies, nor did they, but much propaganda was put out in favour of the proposal. See Philip Noel-Baker, *The Arms Race* (London: Stevens & Sons, 1959) pp. 12–30; and Bundy, *Danger and Survival*, pp. 287–305. The Soviet Union probably played similar games, but they are harder to document.

38. Lawrence Freedman, *The Evolution of Nuclear Strategy* (London: Macmillan Press, 1981) p. 195.

39. Jane Sharp, 'Conventional arms control in Europe: problems and prospects', *SIPRI Yearbook 1988: World Armaments and Disarmament* (SIPRI/Oxford: Oxford University Press, 1988) p. 322.

7   The Present Position and the Policy Alternatives

1. See Alexei Arbatov, 'Military Doctrines', Chapter 11, *Disarmament and Security, 1987 Yearbook* (Moscow, USSR: Institute of World Economy and International Relations, Novosti Press Agency Publishing House, 1988) pp. 214–15; and Marshal Sergei F. Akhromeyev, *Olof Palme Memorial Lecture 1988*, SIPRI, Stockholm (1988) p. 12.

2. Reply, dated 16 November 1987, from Mr Gorbachev to a letter from four members of the Pugwash Study Group on Conventional forces in Europe, Messrs Albrecht von Müller (West Germany), Frank von Hippel (United States), Anders Boserup (Denmark) and the author. For the text, see *Journal of the American Scientists*, Vol. 41, No. 2 (February 1988).

3. Arbatov, 'Military Doctrines', pp. 215–16.

4. Press Release PR 56587 (29 May 1987) The USSR Embassy, London, citing a Tass message from Berlin of 29 May 1987, headed 'Warsaw Treaty Political Consultative Committee – Military Doctrine'. For an earlier statement, see Press Release No. 273 (13 June 1986) of the

Permanent Missions of the Soviet Union, citing a Tass message from Budapest of 11 June 1986, headed 'Address of Warsaw Treaty Member States to NATO Member States, to all European Countries with a Programme of Reducing Armed Forces and Conventional Armaments in Europe'.

5. For example, Alexei Arbatov takes issue with two Soviet generals who argue that it is necessary to be able to undertake offensive operations on a scale sufficient to achieve the 'final rout of an enemy', and questions what a final rout means in Europe today. See 'Defence Dilemmas', in Anders Boserup and Robert Neild (eds), *The Foundations of Defensive Defence* (London: Macmillan, 1990).

6. *NATO Documentation*, 'Brussels Declaration on Conventional Arms Control by Ministers at the North Atlantic Council Session', issued as an attachment to the North Atlantic Council Communiqué following the Ministerial Session of 11 and 12 December 1986.

7. 'Conventional Arms Control – Statement Issued by the North Atlantic Council Meeting in Ministerial Session at NATO Headquarters, Brussels, 8th–9th December 1988', Press Communique M–3(88)75, Press Service, NATO, Brussels 1110. Very little was added to this, except the occasional use of the word disarmament alongside the word arms control, in a later statement, 'A Comprehensive Concept of Arms Control and Disarmament Adopted by Heads of State and Government at the Meeting of the North Atlantic Council in Brussels on 29th and 30th May 1989', NATO Information Service, Brussels 1110.

8. It may be suggested that a remedy could be found by widening negotiations. For example, a preliminary treaty might be made to forbid major new deployments while the main treaty was being negotiated; or the main treaty might be widened so as to prevent circumvention of its core provisions after it came into effect; or there might be a general freeze. But an approach along these lines does not bear critical examination. Consider in turn the three remedies suggested here. With the first, the difficulties in the way of making the main treaty would simply be transferred to the making of the preliminary treaty. With the second, the problem of making the main treaty would be widened without limit since every time another item was included a new frontier would be created beyond which there was another item which called for inclusion. With the third remedy – a general freeze – the problems of deciding what was to be frozen and what a freeze meant (Are replacements of broken weapons to be permitted? And what is to happen to arms factories during the period of the freeze?) would provide sufficient grist to the mill of negotiators to keep them busy for years – if, as the nature of the approach implies, they pursued the negotiation of a freeze in an adversarial spirit.

9. Francois Heisbourg, 'The three ages of NATO strategy', *NATO Review*, Vol. 37 (Brussels, February 1989).

10. See Georgy Arbatov, 'Glasnost, Talks and Disarmament', in Anders Boserup and Robert Neild (eds), *The Foundations of Defensive Defence*.

Appendix: Disarmament Negotiations Before 1945

1. For an excellent short introduction to the subject see, James Joll, *The Origins of the First World War* (London and New York: Longman, 1984). For a lively portrayal of the period, including in particular the atmosphere surrounding the Hague Conferences, see Barbara Tuchman, *The Proud Tower: A Portrait of the World before the War. 1890—1914* (London: Hamish Hamilton, 1966).
2. For an analysis of the shifting balance of world forces, see Paul M. Kennedy, 'The First World War and the International Power System', *International Security*, Vol. 9, No. 1 (Summer 1984) pp. 7–40.
3. Michal Vyvyan, 'The Approach of the War of 1914', *New Cambridge Modern History*, Vol. XII (Cambridge: Cambridge University Press, 1968) p. 152.
4. Brian Bond, 'The First World War', *New Cambridge Modern History*, Vol. XII (Cambridge: Cambridge University Press, 1968) p. 171.
5. Joll, *The Origins of the First World War*, p. 61.
6. Thus Wallach says of 1914, 'Neither side knew how to handle the problem of defence. They simply were not adjusted to it' and 'Nobody can deny that German military doctrine prior to 1914 was pre-occupied with the offensive', Jehuda L. Wallach, *The Dogma of the Battle of Annihilation: The Theories of Clausewitz and Schlieffen and their Impact on the German Conduct of Two World Wars* (Westport, Conn. and London: Greenwood Press, 1986), pp. 160–1.
7. Main sources: Sir Basil Liddell Hart, 'French Military Ideas before the First World War', in Martin Gilbert (ed.), *A Century of Conflict, 1850–1950 – Essays in Honour of A. J. P. Taylor* (London: Hamish Hamilton, 1966); Michael Howard, 'Men Against Fire: The Doctrine of the Offensive in 1914', in Peter Paret (ed.) *Makers of Modern Strategy* (Oxford: Oxford University Press, 1986) pp. 510–26; Michael Geyer, 'German Strategy in the Age of Machine Warfare 1914–45', in Peter Paret (ed.), *Makers in Modern Strategy* (Oxford: Oxford University Press, 1986) pp. 527–97; Scott D. Sagan, '1914 Revisited: Allies Offense and Instability', *International Security*, Vol. 11, No. 2 (Fall 1986); Stephen van Evera *et al.*, in *Military Strategy of the Origins of the First World War* (Princeton: Princeton University Press, 1985); and an exchange between Jack Snyder and Scott D. Sagan in *International Security*, Vol. 11, No. 3 (Winter 1986–87).
8. Liddell Hart, in Martin Gilbert (ed.), *A Century of Conflict, 1850–1950 – Essays in Honour of A. J. P. Taylor* (London: Hamish Hamilton, 1966) p. 140.
9. Liddell Hart, in Gilbert (ed.) *A Century of Conflict*, p. 140.
10. Lawrence Freedman, *The Evolution of Nuclear Strategy* (London: Macmillan Press, 1981) p. 24.
11. See John Ellis, *The Social History of the Machine Gun* (Croom Helm, 1975); and Major C. H. B. Pridham, *Superiority of Firepower; A Short History of Rifles and Machine Guns* (Hutchinson, 1945). A later example is the refusal of British admirals in the inter-war period to

recognise the importance of aircraft relative to battleships. This caused Liddell Hart to write, 'The blindness of hard-headed sailors to realities that were obvious to a dispassionate observer is only explicable through understanding the place that the "ships of the line" filled in their hearts. A battleship had long been to an admiral what a cathedral is to a bishop', Liddell Hart, *Memoirs*, Vol. 1 (London: Cassell, 1965) p. 326.

12. Merze Tate, *The Disarmament Illusion: The Movement for a Limitation of Armaments to 1907* (New York, 1942) pp. 171–2.

13. I. S. Bloch, *Is War Impossible? An abridgement of The War of the Future in its Technical, Economic and Political Relations,* translated from the Russian (London, 1899). Bloch attributed the increase in firepower to the development of magazine rifles, improved artillery and smokeless powder, not the machine gun. See pp. xviii–xxviii and pp. 1–11.

14. Tate, *The Disarmament Illusion*, pp. 171–3.

15. Erich Brandenburg, *From Bismarck to the World War: A History of German Foreign Policy 1870–1914*, Annie Elizabeth Adams (trans.) (Oxford: Oxford University Press, 1933) p. 271.

16. Arthur J. Marder, *From the Dreadnought to Scapa Flow: The Royal Navy in the Fisher Era, 1904–1919*, Vol. 1, *The Road to War* (London: Oxford University Press, 1961) p. 107.

17. Marder, *The Road to War*, p. 107.

18. Marder, *The Road to War*, p. 23.

19. Marder, *The Road to War*, p. 112–13.

20. Marder, *The Road to War*, p. 430.

21. Marder, *The Road to War*, p. 57.

22. Marder, *The Road to War*, pp. 172–3.

23. Marder, *The Road to War*, p. 123.

24. Marder, *The Road to War*, pp. 182–5.

25. Marder, *The Road to War*, p. 152.

26. Marder, *The Road to War*, pp. 156–9; and Philip Noel-Baker, *The Private Manufacture of Armaments* (London: Gollancz, 1936) pp. 449–510.

27. Marder, *The Road to War*, p. 178.

28. Marder, *The Road to War*, p. 315.

29. Brandenburg, *From Bismark to the World War*, p. 272.

30. Tate, *The Disarmament Illusion*, p. 69.

31. Tate, *The Disarmament Illusion*, p. 162.

32. A brief history of the Hague Conference is David J. Bettez, 'Unfulfilled Initiative: Disarmament Negotiations and the Hague Peace Conferences of 1899 and 1907' *The RUSI Journal*, Vol. 133, No. 3 (Autumn 1988); and a full history with particular attention to the role of the movement for disarmament is Tate, *The Disarmament Illusion*; for an analysis written before the First World War by a member of the United States delegation, see Frederick W. Holls, *The Peace Conference at the Hague and its Bearing on International Law and Policy* (London: Macmillan, 1914).

33. Holls, *The Peace Conference*, pp. 8–10.

34. Joll, *The Origins of the First World War*, pp. 174–5.

35. Joll, *The Origins of the First World War*, p. 175.

36. Holls, *The Peace Conference*, p. 377.
37. Bettez, 'Unfulfilled Initiative', p. 60.
38. R. Butler, 'The Peace Settlement of Versailles, 1918–33', in C. L. Mowat (ed.), *Cambridge New Modern History*, Vol. XII (Cambridge: Cambridge University Press, 1968) p. 220.
39. Such was the mistrust between the two countries that in Britain it was argued that the Royal Air Force should be expanded to match France's allegedly more powerful air force. See Barry D. Powers, *Strategy Without Slide-Rule: Britain's Air Strategy 1914–1939* (London: Croom Helm, 1976) pp. 186–7.
40. Buck-passing has been offered as one reason why France failed to extend the Maginot Line along her frontier with Belgium when Belgium in 1936, fearful of Hitler, withdrew into neutrality *vis-à-vis* France. The gap in defences, so runs the argument, would help to draw Britain into any war since she would always try to prevent the Low Countries falling into hostile hands. See Barry R. Posen, *The Sources of Military Doctrine* (Cornell University Press, 1984) pp. 113–16.
41. See Butler, 'The Peace Settlement of Versailles, 1918–1933', p. 238; and J. L. Brierly, 'The League of Nations', in C. L. Mowat (ed.), *Cambridge New Modern History*, Vol. XII, p. 247; and P.J. Noel-Baker, *Disarmament* (The Hogarth Press, 1926) pp. 26–36, 331.
42. Rohan Butler, 'The Peace Settlement of Versailles, 1918–33', pp. 238–40.
43. For the provisions of this treaty see Noel-Baker, *Disarmament*, pp. 103–6.
44. F. P. Walters, *A History of the League of Nations* (London: Oxford University Press, 1952) pp. 228–9.
45. Brierly, 'The League of Nations', p. 247.
46. For general histories of these attempts at disarmament, see Salvador de Madariaga, *Disarmament* (Oxford: Oxford University Press, 1929); and John W. Wheeler-Bennett, *The Disarmament Deadlock* (London: Routledge & Sons, 1934); and Royal Institute of International Affairs, annual *Survey of International Affairs* , for the years 1930 to 1933 (Oxford: Oxford University Press); and Royal Institute of International Affairs, *Documents on International Affairs*, 1932 (Oxford: Oxford University Press, 1933). For a personal view of the reasons for the failure, written by a participant long after the conference, see Philip Noel-Baker, *The First World Disarmament Conference and Why it Failed* (Oxford: Pergamon Press, 1979). For an analysis of the problems encountered in trying to define offensive weapons, see Marion William Boggs, *Attempts to Define and Limit 'Aggressive' Armament in Diplomacy and Strategy* (Columbia: University of Missouri Press, 1941).
47. See Noel-Baker, *Disarmament*, pp. 290–301.
48. Liddell Hart, *Memoirs*, Vol. 1, p. 186.
49. Viscount Cecil of Chelwood (Lord Robert Cecil), *A Great Experiment* (London: Jonathan Cape, 1941) pp. 214–15.
50. Lord Robert Cecil spoke in February 1932 as President of the World Federation of League of Nations Societies. The British Labour Government, for whom Cecil had been delegate to the Preparatory Disarma-

ment Commission – out of devotion to the cause of disarmament not devotion to socialism – had fallen shortly before the conference began and been replaced by a coalition 'National' government.

51. See Royal Institute of International Affairs, *Survey of International Affairs 1932*, p. 221.
52. League of Nations Publications 1932 IX 45, 1932 IX 46, 1932 IX 47, and 1932 IX 48. See also Liddell Hart, *Memoirs*, Vol. 1, p. 209; and *Survey of International Affairs, 1932*, p. 228.
53. *Survey of International Affairs, 1932*, p. 233.
54. In the Kellogg Pact of 1928, fifteen nations, including Britain (with imperial reservations), France, Germany, Italy and the United States, unable to agree on any more concrete means of safeguarding security, rather nebulously renounced war as an instrument of policy. See *Documents on International Affairs, 1928*, pp. 1–14. Other countries later joined, bringing the number to 65 by 1933,
55. *Survey of International Affairs, 1932*, pp. 239–40
56. de Madariaga, *Disarmament,* p. 60.
57. Allen W. Dulles, 'Progress towards Disarmament', *Foreign Affairs* (October 1932).
58. Major-General J. F. C. Fuller, 'What is an Aggressive Weapon?', *The English Review*, LIV (1931) pp. 601–5.
59. Liddell Hart, 'Aggression and the Problem of Weapons', *The English Review*, LV (1932) p. 73.
60. Liddell Hart, 'Aggression and the Problem of Weapons', p. 73.

Index

Index